Kirk Munroe

Canoemates

A story of the Florida Reef and Everglades

Kirk Munroe

Canoemates
A story of the Florida Reef and Everglades

ISBN/EAN: 9783744749329

Printed in Europe, USA, Canada, Australia, Japan

Cover: Foto ©Andreas Hilbeck / pixelio.de

More available books at **www.hansebooks.com**

CANOEMATES

A STORY

OF THE FLORIDA REEF AND EVERGLADES

BY

KIRK MUNROE

AUTHOR OF
"THE FLAMINGO FEATHER" "DERRICK STERLING"
"DORYMATES" "CAMPMATES" ETC.

ILLUSTRATED

NEW YORK
HARPER & BROTHERS, FRANKLIN SQUARE
1893

Copyright, 1892, by HARPER & BROTHERS.

All rights reserved.

CONTENTS.

CHAPTER	PAGE
I. IN THE FAR SOUTH	1
II. THREE CANOES, AND THE FATE OF ONE	8
III. SUMNER RECEIVES A SECOND OFFER	18
IV. TEACHING A THIEF A LESSON	26
V. THE GREAT FLORIDA REEF	33
VI. PINEAPPLES AND SPONGES	41
VII. MYSTERIOUS DISAPPEARANCE OF THE CANOES	49
VIII. LIFE ON THE LONELY ISLAND	57
IX. THE NOCTURNAL VISITOR	64
X. WHOSE ARE THEY? AND WHERE DID THEY COME FROM?	73
XI. SUMNER DRIFTS AWAY ON A RAFT	80
XII. PICKED UP IN THE GULF STREAM	89
XIII. A MYSTERY OF THE REEF	96
XIV. WORTH AND QUORUM ARE MISSING	105
XV. WORTH AND QUORUM IN SEARCH OF SUMNER	112
XVI. A NIGHT IN ALLIGATOR LIGHT	121
XVII. AN ENTERTAINMENT ON THE KEY	128
XVIII. OFF FOR THE EVERGLADES	137
XIX. THE CANOES ARE AGAIN LOST, AND AGAIN FOUND	145
XX. THE PSYCHE AS A LIFE-BOAT	153

Contents.

CHAPTER		PAGE
XXI.	SUMNER'S SELF-SACRIFICE	160
XXII.	GOOD-BYE TO THE TRANSIT	168
XXIII.	WORTH MEETS A PANTHER	175
XXIV.	RATTLESNAKES AND RIFLE-SHOTS	184
XXV.	WORTH'S LONELY NIGHT-WATCH	192
XXVI.	THE FLORIDA EVERGLADES	201
XXVII.	A PREHISTORIC EVERGLADE MOUND	209
XXVIII.	WHAT BECAME OF QUORUM AND THE CANOES	218
XXIX.	A VERY SERIOUS PREDICAMENT	226
XXX.	QUORUM AS AN AMBASSADOR	234
XXXI.	A CLOSELY GUARDED CAMP	242
XXXII.	CROSSING THE 'GLADES WITHOUT SEEING THEM	250
XXXIII.	AN ADVENTUROUS DEER-HUNT	258
XXXIV.	HEMMED IN BY A FOREST FIRE	266
XXXV.	THE BOYS IN A SEMINOLE CAMP	275
XXXVI.	ONE OF THE RAREST ANIMALS IN THE WORLD	284
XXXVII.	FISHING FOR SHARKS	292
XXXVIII.	LITTLE KO-WIK-A SAILS OUT TO SEA	301
XXXIX.	A BLACK SQUALL AND THE STRANDED STEAMER	308
XL.	THE HAPPY ENDING OF THE CRUISE	317

ILLUSTRATIONS.

SUMNER AT HOME	*Frontispiece.*	
"WITH THE NEXT SEND OF THE SEA THE CANVAS CANOE WAS CRUSHED BENEATH THE PONDEROUS BOWS"	*Facing p.*	18
"HE RETURNED TO THE BUOY, ON WHICH THE RECENT FUGITIVE WAS NOW SITTING"	"	30
THE "CUPID" AND "PSYCHE" START ON THEIR CRUISE	"	32
TORCH-FISHING FOR MULLET	"	40
THE CANOES ARE GONE	"	48
"'SOME ONE WAS TRYING TO PULL MY GUN AWAY'"	"	64
"THE LATTER WAS ROLLING ON THE GROUND AT THE FOOT OF A COCOANUT-TREE"	"	68
A GREAT DISCOVERY	"	78
QUORUM IS HAPPY	"	84
"TWO PAIRS OF POWERFUL ARMS DRAGGED HIM INTO THE BOAT"	"	94
"AS HE STEPPED ASHORE A PLEASANT-FACED YOUNG MAN ADVANCED TO MEET HIM"	"	108
QUORUM RESIGNS HIMSELF TO FATE	"	126
QUORUM DANCES A BREAK-DOWN	"	136
"HE FOUND RUST NORRIS CROUCHING IN THE LEE OF THE LITTLE DECK-HOUSE"	"	158

REPAIRING THE "PUNKIN SEED"	Facing p.	168
"A VOLLEY OF RIFLE-SHOTS FLASHED AND ROARED FROM THE FOREST"	"	188
"ROUGH-LOOKING CHARACTERS, WHOM HE AT ONCE RECOGNIZED AS SOUTH FLORIDA COWBOYS"	"	200
"HIS WRISTS WERE UNBOUND, AND THE CLOTH THAT ENVELOPED HIS HEAD WAS SNATCHED FROM IT"	"	220
"DIRECTLY AFTERWARDS A CANOE APPEARED AT THE OPENING IN THE BUSHES"	"	240
"THEY WERE SUDDENLY CONFRONTED BY AN INDIAN ARMED WITH A RIFLE"	"	248
"THE ORDEAL OF FIRE LASTED BUT A MINUTE"	"	272
SUMNER AND WORTH IN THE SEMINOLE CAMP	"	282
SUMNER RESCUES KO-WIK-A	"	310
"THE SURPRISE AND DELIGHT OF THE TWO GENTLEMEN CAN BETTER BE IMAGINED THAN DESCRIBED"	"	322

CANOEMATES.

A Story of the Everglades.

Chapter I.

IN THE FAR SOUTH.

"Really, mother, it doesn't seem as though I could stand it any longer! Life in this place isn't worth living, especially when it's a life of poverty, and what people call 'genteel poverty,' as ours is. Our struggle is for bare existence, and there doesn't seem to be any future to it. If you'd only let me go to New York, I'm sure I could do something there that was worth the doing, but I can't do anything here, and I'd almost rather die than live here any longer!" With this Sumner Rankin flung himself into a chair, and his flushed face was as heavily clouded as though life held nothing of hope or happiness for him.

"Why, my dear boy," exclaimed his mother, standing beside him and smoothing his tumbled brown curls with her cool hands, "what is the matter? I never knew you to speak so bitterly before."

Mrs. Rankin still looked so young and pretty that she might almost be taken for an elder sister of the handsome, seventeen-year-old boy over whom she now bent so tenderly.

To the casual observer the Rankins' home was a very pleasant one. It was a pretty, broad-verandaed cottage nestled in the shadows of a clump of towering cocoanut palms, on the far southern island of Key West. It stood on the outskirts of the town, and so close to the beach that the warm waters of the Mexican Gulf rippling on the coral rocks behind it made a ceaseless melody for its inmates. Jasmine-vines clambered over it, glossy-leaved myrtles, a hedge of night-blooming cereus and other sweet-scented tropical shrubs perfumed the air about it. Through these, looking out from the shaded coolness of the verandas, the eye caught fascinating glimpses of blue waters with white sails constantly passing, and stately men-of-war swinging idly at their moorings. It looked an ideal home; but even in this tropical Eden there was one very large serpent, besides several that were smaller though almost equally annoying. The big one was poverty, and it held the Rankins in its dread embrace as though with no intention of relaxing it.

Mrs. Rankin was the widow of a naval officer who had been stationed at Key West a few years before. He had sent his wife and only child north to escape a dreadful summer of yellow-fever, while he had stayed and died at his post. Shortly before his death Commander Rankin, believing that Key West property was about to increase rapidly in value, had invested all that he had in the little jasmine-clad cottage, expecting to be able to sell it at a handsome profit when his term of service at that station should expire. Thus it was all that remained to his family, and to this haven Mrs. Rankin, sad-eyed and wellnigh broken-hearted, had returned with her boy. The fever had caused real estate to become of so little value that there was no chance of selling the cottage; so they were forced to live in it, and the widow eked out her scanty pension by letting such rooms as she could spare to lodgers. During the pleasant winter season she rarely had difficulty in filling them, but through the long, hot summer months desirable lodgers were few and far between, and the poverty serpent enfolded them closely.

One of the lesser serpents against which the Rankins had to contend was the lack of congenial society; for, with the exception of a few government employés and those whose business compels them to live there, the population of Key West is composed of spongers and wreckers, Cuban and negro cigar-makers. Another was the lack of good schools, and the worst of all was the lack of suitable business openings for Sumner, or "Summer," as his Chinese nurse had called him when he was a baby, and as he had been called ever since on account of his bright face and sunny disposition. He would have loved dearly to go through the Naval Academy and follow the profession that had been his father's, but the Rankins had no political influence, and without that there was no chance. He could not go into a cigar-factory, and though his boyish love of adventure had led him to take several trips on sponging vessels, it was not the business for a gentleman.

Born in China, the boy had, with his mother, followed his naval father to many of the principal ports of the world. Both his father and mother had devoted all their spare time to his education, and thus he was well informed in many branches of which the average boy knows little or nothing. He loved the sea and everything connected with it. From his babyhood he had played with and sailed boats. Now there was no better sailor in Key West than he, nor one more at home among the reefs of those southern waters. He knew the secrets of boat-building from keel to truck, and from stem to stern, while his favorite employment was the whittling out of models, the drawing of sail plans, and the designing of yachts. But nobody wanted yachts in Key West, nor did its sailors care to have improved models for their fishing-boats or sponge-vessels. So Sumner was considered a dreamer, and people said he ought to be doing something besides whittling and idling about home. The boy thought so himself, but what to do and how to set about it were problems the attempted solution of which caused him many an unhappy hour.

On the perfect winter day that he had come home in such a despairing frame of mind, his own life had just been presented in vivid contrast to that of another boy who seemed to have the very things that Sumner most longed for. He had been down to the wharf to see the *Olivette*, the West Indian fast mail-steamer from Tampa, come in. There he had been particularly attracted by a boy somewhat younger than himself, standing with a gentleman, whom Sumner supposed to be his father, on the after-deck. As the steamer neared the wharf this boy amused himself by flinging silver coins into the water for the fun of seeing little negroes dive after them.

"Only think, mother!" exclaimed Sumner in relating this incident, "he threw money away as I would so many pebbles, and didn't seem to value it any more. Just imagine a boy having money to waste like that! And some of those little rascals who dived for it made more in a few minutes than I have to spend in months."

"But, Sumner," said Mrs. Rankin, gravely, "I hope your unhappiness does not arise from jealousy of another's prosperity?"

"Yes, it does, mother," replied the boy, honestly; "though it isn't only because he could throw money away; it is because he has the very thing that I would rather have than anything else in the world—the prettiest, daintiest, cedar sailing canoe that ever was built. I never saw one before, but I've read of them, and studied their plans until I know all about them. She is as different from my old canvas thing as a scow is from a yacht."

"But you thought your canvas canoe very nearly perfect when you built her."

"I know I did, but I have learned better since then, and now it seems as though I should never care to look at it again."

Yet this same despised canvas canoe, which

Sumner had built himself the year before without ever having seen one, had been considered both by himself and his friends a masterpiece of naval construction, and he had cruised in her ever since with great satisfaction.

"You have yet to learn, dear, that it is ever so much harder to be satisfied with the things we have than to obtain those for which we long, no matter how far beyond our reach they may seem," said Mrs. Rankin, gently.

"I suppose it is, mother, and I know it is horrid to come to you with my miserable complainings; but I wish I had never seen those canoes— for there were two of them just alike—and I wish wealthy people wouldn't come to Key West with such things. They don't do us any good, and only make us feel our poverty the more keenly. Why, there they are now! Turning in here too! What can they want with us, I wonder? I won't see them at any rate. I've no more use for wealthy snobs than they have for me."

So saying, Sumner left the room by a rear door, and the steps of the approaching visitors sounded on the front veranda.

Chapter II.

THREE CANOES, AND THE FATE OF ONE.

As Sumner's mother opened the door, she saw that the gentleman who, politely lifting his hat, asked if she were Mrs. Rankin, was too young to be the father of the boy by his side.

"May I introduce myself as Mr. Tracy Manton, of New York?" he said, when she had answered his question in the affirmative; "and my nephew, Master Worth Manton? We have called to see if we can engage rooms here for a week or so. We will take our meals at the hotel; but we have two canoes that we propose fitting out here for a cruise up the reef, and we want to find a place close to the water where we can keep them in safety, and at the same time be near them. Mr. Merrill advised us to come here, and it looks as though this were exactly the place of which we are in search. So if you can accommodate us we shall esteem it a great favor."

With the remembrance of Sumner's last words, Mrs. Rankin hesitated a moment before replying; whereupon Mr. Manton added: "I trust you are not going to refuse us, for I have set my heart on coming here, and will gladly pay full hotel rates for the accommodation."

"If my vacant rooms suit you I shall be pleased to let you have them at my regular rate, which is all they are worth," answered the widow, quietly, as she reflected on the poverty which would not allow even a mother's feelings to interfere with honorable bread-winning. "Will you step in and look at them?"

"We are in luck, my boy, and our little expedition has begun most prosperously," said Mr. Tracy Manton an hour later, as he and his nephew sat in one of the two pretty back-rooms that they had engaged, surrounded by their belongings, and looking out on the sparkling waters of the Gulf. On the grass of the palm-shaded back yard, and in plain sight from the windows, lay the two canoes that had so excited Sumner's admiration and envy. They were indeed beauties as they lay there divested of their burlap wrappings, and that they were fresh from the builder's hands was shown by their unscratched varnish and gleaming metal fittings. They were fifteen feet long by thirty inches wide amidships, were provided with folding metal centre-boards, metal drop-rudders, foot-

and-hand steering gear, water-tight compartments fore and aft, and were decked, with the exception of their roomy cockpits. These were surrounded by stout oak coamings three inches high, sharp-pointed, and flaring outward at the forward ends, but cut down so as to be flush with the deck aft. Beside them lay the confused mass of paddles, sails, spars, canoe tents, rubber aprons, cushions, and cordage, that completed their equipment. They were simply perfect in every detail, and the most beautiful things Sumner Rankin had ever set his eyes upon. At least he thought so, as, returning from a long tramp on which he had tried to walk off his unhappiness, he found them lying in the yard. In spite of his surprise at seeing them there, and a return of his unwelcome feeling of envy, he could not help stopping to admire them and study their details.

"Hello!" exclaimed Mr. Manton, again looking from his window. "There's a chap down there staring his eyes out at our boats. I shouldn't wonder if he were our landlady's son—the one, you know, we were advised to engage as a guide. You wait here while I run down and find out."

So Worth waited and watched from the window to note the result of his uncle's negotiations.

A Story of the Everglades. 11

At a first glance one would have said that Worth Manton was an effeminate boy, with a pale face, blue eyes, and fair hair. If, however, the observer looked long enough to note the square chin, the occasional compression of the thin lips, and flash of the eyes, he might form a different opinion. He was the son of Guy Manton, the great Wall Street operator who had made a fortune out of western railroads, and he had all his life been accustomed to lavish luxury. He was rather delicate, and it was largely on his account that his parents had decided to spend a winter at St. Augustine. The boy had taken but slight interest in the gayeties of the Ponce de Leon, nor had he gained any benefit from the chill rain-storms driven in from the ocean by the east winds of midwinter. The doctor had advised his going farther south; and when his uncle Tracy proposed that they make a canoe trip up the great Florida Reef, which lies off the most southerly coast of the United States, Worth had eagerly seconded the proposition, and had finally won the reluctant consent of his parents.

He knew nothing of canoing, nor did his uncle know much more; but the latter was a good yachtsman, and Worth had had some experience of the same kind, so they felt confident they could manage. They intended to devote some time to studying their craft, and learning their possibilities in the waters about Key West; so two canoes, completely equipped, were ordered from the builder by telegraph. Worth's father promised to charter a yacht, sail down the coast in it, and meet them at Cape Florida about the first of April, and the two would-be canoemen started for Key West full of pleasant anticipations.

Sumner Rankin started at being asked if that were his name, for he had not heard Mr. Manton's step on the grass behind him, and answered rather curtly that it was.

"Well," said the young man, plunging into business at once, as was his habit, "I have been told that you are a first-class sailor, as well as a good reef pilot. My nephew and I are going to cruise up the reef, and I should like to engage your services as boatman and guide. I am willing to pay—"

"It makes no difference what you are willing to pay," interrupted Sumner, with flushed cheeks and flashing eyes. "My services as boatman are not for hire at any price."

With this assertion of his pride, or, as he imagined, of his independence, the boy turned and walked into the house.

A Story of the Everglades.

"Whew!" whistled Mr. Manton, gazing after the retreating form in amazement. "There's a bit of dynamite for you! Pride and poverty mixed in equal parts do make a most powerful explosive. However, I haven't forgotten my own days of poverty, and can fully appreciate the boy's feelings. I'll try him on a different tack as soon as this little squall has blown over. He and his mother must be different from the majority of the people down here, for they are the first we have met who don't seem to want to make money out of us."

Mr. Tracy Manton had no idea of giving up his purpose of engaging Sumner to accompany them on their trip, for he was the kind of a man who wins his way by sticking to whatever plan he has decided upon, in which respect his nephew Worth strongly resembled him. So the next time he met the lad, which was in the afternoon of the following day, he held out his hand and said : " I beg your pardon for my unintentional rudeness of yesterday, and my forgetfulness of the fact that a gentleman is such, no matter where he is found. Now, I want you to forgive me, forget my offence, and do me a favor. I can't make head or tail of our sails, and they don't seem to me right somehow. If you will come and look at them I shall be greatly obliged."

By this time Sumner was so heartily ashamed of his conduct of the day before that he was only too glad to accept this overture of friendship, and a few minutes later the two were busily discussing the sails of the *Cupid* and *Psyche*, as the Mantons' canoes were named. The spars were much heavier than they need be, while the sails were of the ill-shaped, unserviceable pattern generally furnished by canoe builders, and these defects were quickly detected by Sumner's experienced eye. When he pointed them out to Mr. Manton, the latter readily comprehended them, but was at a loss how to make the improvements that were evidently demanded.

In order to explain more thoroughly the idea that he wished to convey, Sumner dragged out his own canvas canoe, stepped her masts, and hoisted her sails. They were of a most ingenious and effective lateen pattern, such as Mr. Manton had never before seen.

"Where did you get hold of that idea?" he asked, after studying them carefully a few moments. "It is a capital one."

"I got it partly from an Arab dhow that I once saw off Madagascar, and partly from the feluccas at Civita Vecchia."

"Madagascar and the Mediterranean!" repeated Mr. Manton, in astonishment. "If you have visited both of those places you must have travelled extensively."

"Yes," answered Sumner, quietly, but with a twinkle of amusement in his eye. "The son of a naval officer who attempts to follow his father about the world is apt to see a good bit of it before he gets through."

Mr. Manton, who had known nothing of Sumner's history, no longer wondered that he had been offended at being taken for a boatman whose services could be hired. He was, however, too wise to make further mention of the subject, and merely said,

"Then you have had a splendid chance to study sails." And again turning to the subject under consideration, he asked, "Would you be willing to help us cut out some for our canoes after your models?"

Sumner answered that he would not only be willing but glad to lend every aid in his power towards properly equipping the two canoes for their trip.

In the mean time the sun had set, and the sky was black with an approaching squall that caused them to watch with some uneasiness for Worth's return. He had gone out in one of the canoes, an hour before, for a paddle, and had not since been seen. Just as the storm broke he appeared around a point and headed towards the little landing-place near which they were standing. As his course lay directly in the teeth of the wind, his struggle was long and hard. They watched him anxiously, and more than once Sumner offered to go to the boy's assistance; but his uncle said he wished Worth to learn self-reliance more than anything else, and this was too good a lesson to be spoiled. Finally the young paddler conquered, and, reaching the landing-place in safety, sprang ashore. He was either too exhausted or too careless to properly secure his canoe, and as he stepped from it a spiteful gust of wind struck it full on the side. In another moment it was beyond reach and drifting rapidly out to sea.

Both the Mantons were confused by the suddenness of the mishap. Before they could form any plan for the recovery of the runaway, Sumner had shoved his own canvas canoe into the water, jumped aboard, and was dashing away in pursuit of the truant. He was almost within reach of his prize, and his tiny sail was almost indistinguishable amid the blackness of the squall, when the watchers on shore were horrified to see another and much larger sail come rushing down, dead before the wind, directly towards it. Then the tiny canoe sail disappeared; and as the larger one seemed to sweep over the spot where it had been, the Mantons gazed at each other with faces that betokened the dread they dared not put into words.

Chapter III.

SUMNER RECEIVES A SECOND OFFER.

For a few minutes Sumner Rankin's peril was most imminent. He was almost within reach of the drifting canoe, which he had been watching too closely to take note of any other object, when he became conscious of the clumsy, wood-laden schooner rushing down on him before the squall. She was manned by a crew of two negroes, and by the manner in which she yawed, heading one moment this way and the next another, he saw that they had but little control of her movements. In vain did he shout to them to look out. His voice was lost in the shriek of the wind, and they did not hear him. He tried to cross their bows, and might have succeeded in so doing, but at that moment their main-sail gybed over with a crash, and the heavy craft, looking as large as a man-of-war in comparison with his cockle-shell, headed directly for him. With the next send of the sea the canvas canoe was crushed beneath the ponderous bows, and blotted from existence as though it had been a drifting leaf.

"WITH THE NEXT SEND OF THE SEA THE CANVAS CANOE WAS CRUSHED BENEATH THE PONDEROUS BOWS."

A Story of the Everglades.

As Sumner saw the black mass towering above him, and before it could descend, he rose to his feet, and taking a straight header, dived deep into the angry waters. When he again came to the surface he was swimming in the foaming wake of the schooner, and drifting down towards him from the windward was the beautiful cedar canoe which was the cause of all the trouble, and which he had passed in his effort to save his own from destruction. A few strokes took him to her, and with a feeling of devout thankfulness he clutched her gunwale.

Worth Manton, or any other inexperienced canoeman, would have attempted to climb up over the bow or stern, and, sitting astride the slippery deck, to work his way into the cockpit. Such an attempt would have been almost certain to roll the light craft over and fill her with water, in which case she would become wholly unmanageable. But Sumner knew better than to do such a thing. He had practised capsizing so often in his crank canvas canoe that to get into this comparatively broad-beamed and stable craft was the easiest kind of a performance. Seizing hold of the coaming directly amidship, he placed his left hand on the side of the cockpit nearest him, and reaching far over, grasped the other side with his right. Then kicking in the water behind him until his body lay nearly flat on its surface, and bearing as much weight as possible on his right hand, he drew himself squarely across the cockpit, and in another moment was seated in it, without having shipped a drop of water over the coaming.

There was no paddle in the canoe, and though she rode the waves like a cork, she was entirely at the mercy of the wind and tide. Although the squall was passing, the darkness of night was rapidly shutting out all familiar objects, and Sumner was on the point of resigning himself to a night of aimless drifting, with an interesting uncertainty as to when he should be picked up, when a distant shout, that sounded exceedingly like his own name, was borne to his ears. He sent back an answering cry, the shout was repeated, and a few minutes later the shadowy form of the *Psyche*, with Mr. Manton wielding a double-bladed paddle, shot out of the darkness.

"I never was so glad to find any one in my life!" exclaimed the new-comer. "We were afraid that clumsy schooner had run you down. I tell you what, boy, the last ten minutes have been the most anxious I ever passed, and I wouldn't go through with them again for all the canoes in the world. But what has become of your own boat?"

"She has gone to the bottom, like many a good ship before her," replied Sumner; "and it wasn't the fault of those lubbers on the schooner that I didn't go with her. Have you an extra paddle with you?"

"No; I neglected to bring one, and I shall have to take you in tow."

They had already drifted down past the fort that commands the harbor from the south-west point of the island, and as they could not hope to make their way back against wind and tide, they were compelled to work in behind it, and make a landing on the south beach a mile or more from where they started. Here Mr. Manton remained in charge of the canoes, while Sumner ran home to announce his own safety, obtain a change of clothing and another paddle.

He found his mother and Worth in a terrible state of anxiety concerning him; but he made so light of his recent adventure that it was not until after the canoes were brought safely back, an hour later, that they learned the full extent of his recent peril.

This incident seemed to cement a firm friendship between Sumner and the Mantons, and while the former stubbornly refused to accept the recompense for his lost canoe that Mr. Manton tried to force upon him, declaring that it was only his own carelessness in not keeping a sharper lookout, the latter made up his mind that, in spite of his pride, the boy must and should be rewarded in some way for what he had done.

The following week was busily and happily spent in making new sails for the two canoes, rerigging them, and in teaching Worth how to manage his. It struck Sumner as a little curious that, even after the new sails were made, Mr. Manton was always too busy to go out on these practice trips with his nephew, and invariably asked him to take the *Psyche* and act as instructor in his place. Of course he could not refuse to do this, nor did he have the slightest inclination to do so; for what boy who loved boats would not have jumped at the chance of sailing that dainty craft? How Sumner did appreciate her speed and seaworthy qualities! He raced with every sponger and fisherman in the harbor, and caused their eyes to open with amazement at the ease with which he beat them. How fond he became of the canoe that bore him to so many victories! How, with all his heart, he did wish he were going in her on the cruise up the reef, for which such extensive preparations were being made! Much as he wished this, however, he was very careful not to express the wish to any person except his mother, to whom he always confided all his hopes, fears, and plans. After his refusal of Mr. Manton's offer to accompany them as guide, he would not for anything have let that gentleman know how eagerly he longed to have the offer repeated in such form that his pride would allow him to accept it. Still, as he had no canoe now, it would be impossible for him to go, and there was no use in thinking of it.

So he tried to make the most of his present opportunities, and gain all the pleasure that they held. Nor did he neglect Worth, but instructed him so thoroughly in the art of canoe-handling, that at the end of a week the boy was as much at home in his canoe as he had ever been on a yacht.

One day, as the two beautiful craft, with their perfect setting lateen-sails, were glancing in and out among the anchored sponge fleet on the north side of the island, like white-winged sea-birds, a young sponger, named Rust Norris, called out from one of the boats, "Say, Sumner, come here a minute, will yer?"

As the latter sailed alongside and asked what he wanted, the sponger answered: "I want to try that fancy trick of yourn. Let me take her a few minutes, will yer?"

"No," replied Sumner; "I can't, because she

isn't mine to lend. Besides, as you are not accustomed to this style of craft, you couldn't sail her, anyhow; and you'd upset before you had gone a length."

"Oh, I would, would I? Well, I'll bet I can sail anything you can, or any other landlubber that thinks he knows it all because his daddy belonged to the navy."

Then, as Sumner, with a flushed face, but disdaining any reply, sheered off and sailed away, he added, "I'd jest naturally hate myself if I was as mean as you be, Sumner Rankin, and I won't forget your disobligingness in a hurry, neither!"

In the mean time Mr. Manton had studied Sumner's character carefully, and the more he did so the more he was pleased with the boy. He found him to be proud and high-tempered, but also manly, straightforward, and honest to a fault, as well as prompt to act in emergencies, self-reliant, and a thorough sailor. In the course of several conversations with the boy's mother he learned much of Sumner's past history and of his dreams for the future. To her he finally confided a plan, formed on the day that Sumner saved Worth's canoe at the expense of his own, and after some discussion won her assent to it.

It was nothing more nor less than that Sumner should take his place on the proposed cruise up the reef, and act the part of guide, companion, and friend to the younger canoeman.

"I shall not for a second time be guilty of the mistake of trying to hire you to take this cruise," said Mr. Manton, smiling, as he unfolded this plan to Sumner; "but I ask you to do it as a favor to both me and Worth. Indeed, it will be a great favor to me," he added, hastily, as he saw an expression of doubt on the lad's face; "for I really ought to be in New York at this very minute, attending to some important business, which I was only willing to neglect in case Worth could not take this trip without me. Now, however, I am confident that he will be safer with you than he would be with me alone, and if you will take my canoe and accompany him to Cape Florida, where I shall try to meet you about the first of April, you will place me under an obligation. Will you do it?"

Chapter IV.

TEACHING A THIEF A LESSON.

Was there ever such a chance to do the very thing he most longed to do offered a boy before? Sumner did not believe there ever had been, and with a quick glance at his mother's smiling face, in which he read her assent to the plan, he answered:

"I don't know how to thank you, sir, for making me such a splendid offer, and not only will I gladly accept it, but I promise to do everything in my power to make Worth have a good time, and see that no harm befalls him. But I wish you were going too. I hate to think of taking your place and depriving you of all the pleasure of the trip."

"My dear boy," replied Mr. Manton, "you must not look at it in that way, for, as I said before, you will be doing me a real favor in taking my place. I am more of a yachtsman than a canoeman anyway, and I look forward with fully as much pleasure to cruising down the Indian River from St. Augustine in the yacht that my brother proposes to charter, and meeting you at Cape Florida, as I should to running up the reef in a canoe. There is one more thing, however. I must insist upon your sailing your own canoe, for I make it a rule never to lend my boats to any one, and you will have enough responsibility in looking after Worth, without having the added one of caring for another person's canoe. So, from this moment, the *Psyche*, and all that she contains, is yours."

"Oh, Mr. Manton!"

"That will do. Not another word," laughed the young man. "I am as obstinate as a mule when I have once made up my mind to a thing, and so there is nothing for you to do but take the canoe, and make the best use you can of her."

Sumner's protests against this generosity were but feeble ones, and were quickly disposed of by Mr. Manton, who simply refused to listen to them. He cut them short by saying, "Now that this matter is settled, and everything is in readiness for a start, I propose that you get off in the morning, for I want to take to-morrow night's steamer for Tampa."

That night, after everybody had gone to bed and the house was still, Sumner lay wide awake, thinking over the good-fortune that had befallen him. At length he could not resist the temptation of getting up, partly dressing himself, and slipping out for a look at his canoe, his very own! the most beautiful craft he had ever seen, and such a one as in his wildest dreams he had never hoped to possess.

The two canoes had been drawn up on the grass not far from the water's edge, and covered with some bits of old canvas. Although it was a moonlit night, the moon was occasionally obscured by drifting clouds, and when Sumner left the house everything was in shadow from this cause. He moved very quietly, for he did not wish any one to know of the weakness that led him to look at something with which he was already familiar, merely because it had acquired the new interest of possession.

To his amazement, when he reached the place where the canoes had been left, he could find but one of them. In vain did he lift the canvas that had covered them both, and look hurriedly about the little yard. One of them was certainly gone, and no trace of it remained. As the boy stood irresolute, wondering what he ought to do, he was startled by a slight splash in the water. At the same moment the cloud passed from the face of the moon, and by the light thus afforded Sumner saw the figure of a man seated in the missing canoe, and cautiously paddling from the shore.

Without an instant's hesitation he slid the remaining canoe over the grass and into the water, sprang into it, seized a paddle, and started in pursuit. Of course the paddler in the first canoe might be one of the Mantons, but Sumner did not believe it was either of them. He thought it more than likely that the stranger was some one who only desired to try the canoe, but it might be a thief. At any rate, the boy determined to discover who he was, and what he meant by his stealthy performance before they were many minutes older.

The stranger did not realize that he was pursued until Sumner had shoved off from shore, and was urging his own craft forward with vigorous strokes of his double-bladed paddle. When, by a glance over his shoulder, he discovered this, he redoubled his efforts to escape, and by his clumsy splashings proved himself a novice in the art of paddling. Still he made fair headway, and it was not until they were several hundred yards from shore that Sumner overtook him.

Here was anchored an immense mooring-buoy, with a round, slightly conical top, having in its centre a great iron ring. It did not rise more than a foot from the surface of the water, and in trying to watch Sumner, the occupant of the leading canoe did not notice it until his light craft struck it a glancing blow, and very nearly upset. The next instant an effort to recover his equilibrium had precipitated the fellow into the water, and as Sumner shot past him he was wildly clutching at the buoy, with desperate efforts to gain its upper surface.

Satisfied that he could not drown so long as he clung to the buoy, Sumner first picked up the drifting canoe. With it in tow he returned to the buoy on which the recent fugitive was now sitting, clinging tightly to the iron ring, and presenting a comical picture of misery.

"Don't leave me here," Sumner!" he cried, in an imploring tone, in which the boy at once recognized the voice of Rust Norris. "I didn't mean no harm. I only just wanted to try the trick, and I meant to put her back again where I found her. Honest I did!"

"Well, I don't know," replied Sumner, who could not help laughing at the other's plight, in spite of his anger at him for taking the canoe without leave, and his suspicion that it would not have been returned so promptly as Rust claimed it would. "You look quite as comfortable as you deserve to be; besides, you will have a nice quiet chance out here to learn the lesson

"HE RETURNED TO THE BUOY, ON WHICH THE RECENT FUGITIVE WAS NOW SITTING."

that it is better to leave other people's property alone than to take it without permission. So, on the whole, I think I will leave you where you are for a while. I did think of having you arrested for stealing, but I guess this will do just as well."

Thus saying, the boy began to paddle towards shore, and at the same time Rust changed his pleading tone to one of bitter invective, uttering loud threats of what he would make Sumner suffer in the future.

Without paying any attention to these, the young canoeman continued on his way to the shore. From there he watched until he saw the dim form of a fishing-boat come silently drifting down the harbor with the tide. As she neared the spot where he knew the buoy with its unwilling occupant to be, he heard shouts, saw the boat alter her course, and stop for a minute. As she again proceeded, and he was satisfied that his prisoner had been rescued, Summer again went to bed, this time to sleep soundly until morning.

When he related this adventure at breakfast-time, Mr. Manton said he had served the rascal right; but Mrs. Rankin was fearful lest some future mischief should come of it. At this Sumner laughed, and said he thought the lesson would teach Rust Norris to let his things alone in the future, also that he was not afraid of anything the young sponger could do anyhow.

The morning was spent in loading the canoes and in making final preparations for the start. By noon all was in readiness, and after a hasty lunch the two young canoemates stepped aboard their dainty craft. Then, amid a waving of handkerchiefs and a chorus of hearty good-byes from the group of spectators assembled to see them off, they hoisted sail, and bore away on the first reach of what was to prove one of the most eventful and exciting cruises ever undertaken up the Florida Reef.

THE "CUPID" AND "PSYCHE" START ON THEIR CRUISE.

A Story of the Everglades. 33

Chapter V.

THE GREAT FLORIDA REEF.

The great Florida Reef, up which our young canoemates had just started on their adventurous cruise, is about 230 miles long. It extends from Cape Florida, on the Atlantic coast, completely around the southern end of the peninsula, and far out into the Gulf of Mexico on the west. The island of Key West lies some 70 miles off the main-land, and about the same distance from the Dry Tortugas, which group of little coral islets forms the western extremity of the reef. Between Key West, on which is a city of the same name containing nearly 20,000 inhabitants, who live farther south than any one else in the United States, and Cape Florida, 150 miles east and north, a multitude of little keys or islands, covered to the water's edge with a dense growth of mangroves and other tropical trees and shrubs, stretch in a continuous line. Between these keys*

---

* The word "key" is a corruption of the Spanish *Cayo* or island. Thus Key West was originally "Cayo Hueso," or Bone Island, so called from the quantity of human bones found on it by the first white settlers.

and the main-land lies a vast shallow expanse of water known as the Bay of Florida. Outside of them is the narrow and navigable Hawk Channel, running along their entire length, and bounded on its seaward side by the almost unbroken wall of the outer reef. This rarely rises above the surface, and on it the busy coral insects pursue their ceaseless toil of rock-building. Beyond the reef, between it and the island of Cuba, eighty miles away, pours the mighty flood of the Gulf Stream.

For nearly 300 years these peaceful looking keys, with their bewildering net-work of channels, kept open by the rushing tide-currents, and coral reefs were the chosen resorts of pirates and wreckers, both of whom reaped rich rewards from the unfortunate vessels that fell into their hands. Now the pirates have disappeared, and the business of the wreckers has been largely taken from them by the establishment of a range of lighthouses along the outer reef, at intervals of twenty to thirty miles. The first of these is on Loggerhead Key, the outermost of the Tortugas. Then comes Rebecca Shoal, half-way between Loggerhead and Sand Key Light, which is just off Key West. From here the lights in order up the reef are American Shoal, Sombrero, Alligator, Carysfort, and Fowey Rocks, off Cape Florida.

With this chain of flashing beacons to warn mariners of the presence of the dreaded reef, the palmy days of wreckers and beach-combers have passed away, and they must content themselves with what they can make out of the occasional vessels that are still drawn in to the reef by the powerful currents ever setting towards it. Consequently most of those who would otherwise be wreckers have turned their attention to sponging in the waters behind the keys, which form one of the great sponge-fields of the world, or to the raising of pineapples and cocoanuts on such of the islands as afford sufficient soil for this purpose.

There are four ways by which one may sail up the reef. The first is outside in the Gulf Stream, or by "way of the Gulf;" the second is between the reef and the keys, through the Hawk Channel; the third is through the narrow and intricate channels among the keys, or "inside," as the spongers say; and the fourth is the "bay way," or through the shoal waters behind the keys.

Of all these, the third, or inside way, was the one chosen by Sumner as being the most protected from wind and seas, the most picturesque, the one affording the most frequent opportunities for landing, the most interesting, and in every way best adapted to canoes drawing but a few inches of water.

As the *Psyche* and *Cupid* are running easily along the north shore of the key before a light southerly breeze, there is time to take a look at the "duffle" with which they are laden. In the first place, each has two lateen-sails, the long yards of which are hoisted on short masts rising but a few feet from the deck. These sails can be hoisted, lowered, or quickly reefed by the canoeman from where he sits. The two halves of the double-bladed paddles are held in metal clips on deck, on either side of the cockpit. Also on deck, securely fastened, is a small folding anchor, the light but strong five-fathom cable of which runs through a ring at the bow, and back to a cleat just inside the forward end of the coaming.

On the floor of each canoe is folded a small tent made of gay-striped awning-cloth, and provided with mosquito-nettings at the openings. Above these are laid the pair of heavy Mackinaw blankets and the rubber poncho that each carries. These, which will be shelter and bedding at night, answer for seats while sailing.

Under the deck, at one side of each cockpit, hangs a double-barrelled shot-gun; and on the other side are half a dozen tiny lockers, in which

A *Story of the Everglades.*

are stowed a few simple medicines, fishing-tackle, matches, an alcohol lamp (Flamme forcé), loaded shells for the guns, etc. In the after-stowage lockers are extra clothing and toilet articles. The *Psyche* carries the mess-chest, containing a limited supply of table-ware, sugar, coffee, tea, baking-powder, salt, pepper, etc., and a light axe, both of which are stowed at the forward end of the cockpit. The *Cupid* carries in the same place a two-gallon water-keg and a small, but well-furnished tool chest. The provisions, of which bacon, flour, oatmeal, sea-biscuit, a few cans of baked beans and brown bread, dried apples, syrup, cocoa, condensed milk, corn-meal, rice, and hominy form the staples, and the few necessary cooking utensils, which are made to fit within one another, are evenly divided between the two canoes and stowed under the forward hatches. By Sumner's advice, many things that the Mantons brought with them have been left behind, and everything taken along has been reduced to its smallest possible compass. Besides the shot-gun that Mr. Manton had given him as part of the *Psyche's* outfit, Sumner was armed with a revolver that had been his father's.

Late in the afternoon they passed the eastern point of the island of Key West, and crossing a broad open space, in the shoal waters of which, but for Sumner's intimate knowledge of the place, even their light canoes would have run aground a dozen times, they approached the cocoanut groves of Boca Chica, a large key on which they proposed to make their first camp.

The western sky was in a glory of flame as they hauled their craft ashore, and from the tinted waters myriads of fish were leaping in all directions, as though intoxicated by the splendor of the scene.

"We will catch some of those fine fellows a little later," said Sumner, as they began to unload their canoes and carry the things to the spot they had already chosen for a camp.

"But it will be dark," protested Worth.

"So much the better. It's ever so much easier to catch fish in the dark than by daylight."

There was plenty of drift-wood on the beach, and in a few minutes the merry blaze of their camp-fire was leaping from a pile of it. While waiting for it to burn down to a bed of coals, each of them drove a couple of stout stakes, and pitched their canoe tents near a clump of tall palms, just back of the fire, looped up the side openings, and spread their blankets beneath them.

"Now let's fly round and get supper," cried Sumner, "for I am as hungry as a kingfish.

You put the coffee water on to boil, while I cut some slices of bacon, Worth, and then I'll scramble some eggs, too, for we might as well eat them while they are fresh."

With his back turned to the fire, the former did not notice what Worth was doing, until a hissing sound, accompanied by a cry of dismay, caused him to look round.

"I never saw such a miserable kettle as that!" exclaimed Worth. "Just look; it has fallen all to pieces."

For a moment Sumner could not imagine what had caused such a catastrophe. Then he exclaimed: "I do believe you must have set the kettle on the coals before you put the water into it."

"Of course I did," answered Worth, "so as to let it get hot. And the minute I began to pour water into it, it went all to pieces."

"Experience comes high," said Sumner, "especially when it costs us the loss of our best kettle; but we've got to have it at any price, and I don't believe you'll ever set a kettle on the fire again without first putting water or some other liquid inside of it."

"No, I don't believe I will," answered Worth, ruefully, "if that is what happens."

In spite of this mishap, the supper was successfully cooked, thanks to Sumner's culinary knowledge, and by the time it was over and the dishes had been washed, he pronounced it dark enough to go fishing. First he cut a quantity of slivers from a piece of pitch-pine drift-wood, then, having emptied one of the canoes of its contents, he invited Worth to enter it with him.

"But we haven't a single fish-line ready," protested Worth.

"Oh yes, we have," laughed Sumner, lighting one end of the bundle of pine slivers, and giving it to Worth to hold. "You just sit still and hold that. You'll find out what sort of a fish-line it is in a minute. Then he paddled the canoe very gently a few rods off shore, at the same time bearing down on one gunwale until it was even with the surface of the water. "Look out, here they come!" he shouted.

TORCH-FISHING FOR MULLET

Chapter VI.

PINEAPPLES AND SPONGES.

THE next instant Worth uttered a startled cry and very nearly dropped his torch, as a mullet, leaping from the water, struck him on the side of the head, and fell flapping into the canoe.

"Never mind a little thing like that," cried Sumner. "Hold your torch a trifle lower. That's the kind!"

Now the mullet came thick and fast, attracted to the bright light like moths to a candle-flame. They leaped into the canoe and over it, they fell on its decks and flopped off into the water, they struck the two boys until they felt as though they were being pelted with wet snowballs; and at length one of them, hitting the torch, knocked it from Worth's hand, so that it fell hissing into the water.

The effect of this sudden extinguishing of the light was startling. In an instant the fish ceased to jump, and disappeared, while the recent noisy confusion was succeeded by an intense stillness, only broken by an occasional flap from one of the victims to curiosity that had fallen into the canoe.

"Well, that is the easiest way of fishing I ever heard of," remarked Worth, as they stepped ashore, and turning the canoe over, spilled out fifty or more fine mullet. A dozen of them were cleaned, rubbed with salt, and put away for breakfast. Then the tired canoemates turned in for their first night's sleep in camp.

Sumner's eyes were quickly closed, but Worth found his surroundings so novel that for a long time he lay dreamily awake watching the play of moonlight on the rippling water, listening to the splash of jumping fish, the music of little waves on the shell-strewn beach, and the ceaseless rustle of the great palm leaves above him. At length his wakefulness merged into dreams, and when he next opened his eyes it was broad daylight, the sun had just risen, and Sumner was building a fire.

"Hurrah, Worth! Tumble out of bed and tumble into the water," he called at that moment. "There's just time for a dip in the briny before this fire'll be ready for those fish." Suiting his actions to his words, he began pulling off his clothes, and a minute later the two boys were diving into the cool water like a couple of frisky young porpoises.

Oatmeal and syrup, fresh mullet, bread-and-butter (which they had brought from home), and coffee, formed a breakfast that Sumner declared fit for a railroad king.

The sun was not more than an hour high before they were again under way, this time working hard at their paddles, as the breeze had not yet sprung up. Having left their first camp behind them, they felt that their long cruise had indeed begun in earnest.

For the next three days they threaded their way, under sail or paddle, among such numberless keys and through such a maze of narrow channels, that it seemed to Worth as though they were entangled in a labyrinth from which they would never be able to extricate themselves. Whenever a long sand-spit or reef shot out from the north side of one key, a similar obstruction was certain to be found on the south end of the next one. Thus their course was a perpetual zigzag, and a fair wind on one stretch would be dead ahead on the next. Now they slid through channels so narrow that the dense mangroves on either side brushed their decks, and then they would be confronted by a coral reef that seemed to extend unbrokenly in both directions as far as the eye could reach. Worth would make up his mind that there was nothing to do but get out and drag the canoes over it, when suddenly the *Psyche*, which was always in the lead, would dash directly at the obstacle, and skim through one of the narrow cuts with which all these reefs abound.

For a long time it was a mystery to Worth how Sumner always kept in the channel without hesitating or stopping to take soundings. Finally he discovered that it was by carefully noting the color of the water. He learned that white water meant shoals, that of a reddish tinge indicated sand-bars or reefs, black water showed rocks or grassy patches, and that the channels assumed varying shades of green, according to their depth.

They camped with negro charcoal-burners on one key, and visited an extensive pineapple patch on another. Having heard this fruit spoken of as growing on trees, Worth was amazed to find it borne on plants with long prickly leaves that reached but little above his knees. The plants stood so close together, and their leaves were so interlaced, that he did not see how any one ever walked among them to cut the single fruit borne at the head of each one; and when he tried it, stepping high to avoid the bayonet-like leaves, his wonder that any human being could traverse the patch was redoubled.

"I would just as soon try to walk through a field covered with cactus plants," he said.

"So would I," laughed Sumner, "if I had to walk as you do. In a pineapple patch you must never lift your feet, but always shuffle along. In that way you force the prickly leaves before you, and move with their grain instead of against it."

Although the crop would not be ready for cutting much before May, they found here and there a lusciously ripe yellow "pine," and after eating one of these, Worth declared that he had never before known what a pineapple was. He did not wonder that they tasted so different here and in New York, when he learned that for shipment north they must be cut at least two weeks before they are ripe, while they are hard and comparatively juiceless.

At the end of three days an outgoing tide, rushing like a mill-race, swept the canoes through the green expanse of "The Grasses," that looked like a vast submerged meadow, and into the open waters of the Bahia Honda, or, as the reef-men say, the "Bay o' Hundy." Here they first saw spongers at work, and devoted an entire day to studying their operations.

Worth had always supposed that sponges were dived for, but now he learned his mistake. He found that in those waters they are torn from the bottom and drawn to the surface by iron rakes with long curved teeth attached to slender handles from twenty to thirty feet in length. The sponging craft are small sloops or schooners, each of which tows from two to six boats behind it. When a sponge bed is discovered, two men go out in each of these boats. One of them sculls it gently along, while the other leans over the gunwale with a water-glass in his hands, and carefully examines the bottom as he is moved slowly over it. The water-glass is a common wooden bucket having a glass bottom. This is held over the side of the boat so that its bottom is a few inches below the surface of the water, or beyond the disturbing influence of ripples. With his head in this bucket, the sponger gazes intently down until he sees the round black object that he wants. Then he calls out to the sculler to stop the boat, and with the long-handled rake that lies by his side secures the prize. It is black and slimy, and full of animal matter that quickly dies, and decomposes with a most disgusting odor. To this the spongers become so accustomed that they do not mind it in the least, and fail to understand why all strangers take such pains to sail to windward of their boats.

When the deck of a sponge boat is piled high with this unsavory spoil of the sea, she is headed towards the nearest key on which her crew have established a crawl,* and her cargo is tossed into it. The crawl is a square pen of stakes built in the shallow water of some sheltered bay, and in it the sponges lie until their animal matter is so decomposed that it will readily separate from them. Then they are stirred with poles or trodden by the feet of the spongers until they are free from it, when they are taken from the crawl, and spread on a beach to dry and whiten in the sun. When a full cargo has been obtained, they are strung in bunches, and taken to Key West to be sold by the pound at auction. There they are trimmed, bleached again, pressed into bales, and finally shipped to New York.

Sponges are of many grades, of which the sheep's wool is the finest, and the great loggerheads the most worthless. As spongers can only work in water that is smooth, or nearly so, half their time is spent in idleness; and though they receive large prices for what they catch, the average of their wages is low.

One hot afternoon at the end of a week found our canoemates half-way up the reef, and approaching a key called Lignum Vitæ, which is for several reasons one of the most remarkable of all the keys. It is a large island lifted higher

* Crawl is a corruption of corral, meaning a yard or pen.

above the surface of the water than any of the other keys, and it contains in its centre a small fresh-water lake. It is covered with an almost impenetrable forest growth, and concealed by this are ancient stone walls, of which no one knows the origin or date.

Sumner had told Worth so much concerning this key as to arouse his curiosity, and they both looked forward with interest to reaching it. All day they had seen it looming before them, and when they finally dropped sail close beside it, Worth proposed that they take advantage of the remaining daylight to make a short exploration before unloading their canoes and pitching camp. To this Sumner agreed, and as they could not drag the laden boats up over the rocky beach, they decided to anchor them out and wade ashore. So the *Psyche's* anchor was flung out into the channel, the *Cupid* was made fast to her, and a light line from its stern was carried ashore and tied to a tree. Then, taking their guns with them, the boys plunged into the forest.

When, an hour later, they returned from their exploration, bringing with them a brace of ducks and half a dozen doves that they had shot, they gazed about them in bewildered dismay. The canoes were not where they had left them, nor could any trace of them be discovered.

Chapter VII.

MYSTERIOUS DISAPPEARANCE OF THE CANOES.

"THE canoes are gone!" cried Worth.

"It looks like it," replied Sumner, in an equally dismayed tone.

"Are you sure this is where we left them?"

"Yes; sure. There is the stern line that we made fast to the *Cupid*, or what is left of it."

Sure enough, there was a portion of the light line still fast to the tree, and as Sumner pulled it in, both boys bent over to examine it. It had been broken, and not cut. From its length it must also have been broken close to the canoe.

"Oh, Sumner, what shall we do?" asked Worth, in a tone of such despair that the former at once realized the necessity of some immediate action to divert his comrade's thoughts.

"Do?" he cried. "There's plenty to do. First, we'll go down to that point and take a look to seaward; for, as the tide is running out, they are more likely to have gone in that direction than any other. It would be a comfort even to catch a glimpse of them. Then, perhaps, they have only drifted away, and are stranded on some bar near by. Besides looking for the canoes, we must build some kind of a shelter for the night, cook supper, and discuss our plans for the future. Oh yes, we've plenty to do!"

While he spoke, the boys were making their way to the point in question, and when they reached it, they eagerly scanned every foot of water in sight. Diagonally to the right from where they stood stretched the long reach of Lower Metacumba, desolate and uninhabited as they knew. Almost directly in front, but several miles away, rose the palm-crowned rocks of Indian Key, with its two or three old shed-like buidings in plain view. These had been used and abandoned years before by the builders of Alligator Light, the slender tower of which they could see rising from the distant waters above the outer reef. Diagonally on the left was the tiny green form of Tea Table Key, and dimly beyond it they could make out the coast of Upper Metacumba, which Sumner said was inhabited. In all this far-reaching view, however, there were no signs of the missing canoes.

"I'm glad of it!" said Sumner, after his long searching gaze had failed to reveal them. "It would be rough to have them in sight but out of reach."

A Story of the Everglades. 51

Already the sun was sinking behind the tree-tops of Lower Metacumba, fish were leaping in the placid waters, and a few pelican were soaring with steady poise above them. Every now and then these would swoop swiftly down, with a heavy splash that generally sealed the fate of one or more mullet off which the great birds were making their evening meal. A flock of black cormorants, uttering harsh cries, flew overhead with a rushing sound, returning from a day's fishing to their roosts in the distant Everglades. With these exceptions, and the faint boom of the surf on the outer reef, all was silence and desertion. Besides the light-house tower there was no sign of human life, not even the distant glimmer of a sail. While the boys still looked longingly for some trace of their canoes, the sun set, and a red flash, followed at short intervals by two white ones, shot out from the vanishing form of Alligator Light.

"Come!" cried Sumner, heedful of this warning. "Night is almost here, and we have too much to do in every precious minute of twilight to be standing idle. I'll take the bucket and run to the pond for water, while you cut all the palmetto leaves you possibly can, and carry them to the place where we landed."

"The bucket?" repeated Worth, looking about

him inquiringly. "Where are you going to find it?"

Without answering, Sumner sprang down the rocks to the water's edge, where he had noticed a stranded bamboo, and quickly cut out a short section of it with the hatchet that he had thrust into his belt before leaving the canoes. As he made the cuts just below two of the joints, his section was a hollow cylinder, open at one end, but having a tight bottom and capable of holding several quarts of water. With this he plunged into the forest in the direction of the pond, handing Worth the hatchet as he passed, and bidding him be spry with his palmetto leaves.

A few minutes later, as Sumner emerged from the trees, carrying his full water-bucket, and breathless with his haste, he indistinctly saw the form of some animal at the very place where they had left their guns and birds. As the boy dashed forward, uttering a loud cry, the alarmed animal scuttled off into the bushes.

"Oh, you vil-li-an!" gasped Sumner as he reached the place, "I'll settle with you to-morrow, see if I don't."

Four of the doves had disappeared, and the head was torn from one of the ducks.

"What is it?" cried Worth, in alarm, as he entered the clearing from the opposite side, staggering beneath an immense load of cabbage-palm leaves.

"A rascally thieving 'coon," answered Sumner, "and he has got away with the best part of our provisions, too; but I'll get even with him yet. Now give me the hatchet, and then pick up all the drift-wood you can find, while I build a house."

Worth would gladly have helped erect the house, as Sumner called it, for he was very curious as to what sort of a structure could be built of leaves, but he realized the necessity of doing as he was bidden, and at once set to work gathering wood. Sumner, after carefully propping his water-bucket between two rocks, so as to insure the safety of its contents, began cutting a number of slender saplings, and turning them into poles. The stoutest of these he bound with withes to two trees that stood about six feet apart. He fastened it to their trunks as high as he could reach. Then he bound one end of the longer poles to it, allowing them to slant to the ground behind. Crosswise of these, and about a foot apart, he tied a number of still more slender poles, and over these laid the broad leaves. He would have tied these securely in place if he had had time. As he had not, for it was quite dark before he finished even this rude shelter, he was forced to leave them so, and hope that a wind would not arise during the night. For himself alone he would not have built any shelter, but would have found a comfortable resting-place under a tree. Knowing, however, that Worth had never in his life slept without a roof of some kind above him, he thought it best to provide one, and thereby relieve their situation of a portion of the terror with which the city-bred boy was inclined to regard it.

It was curious and interesting to note how a sense of responsibility, and the care of one younger and much more helpless than himself, was developing Sumner's character. Already the selfishness to which he was inclined had very nearly disappeared, while almost every thought was for the comfort and happiness of his companion. Worth, accustomed to being cared for and having every wish gratified, hardly appreciated this as yet; but the emergencies of their situation were teaching him valuable lessons of prompt obedience and self-reliance that he could have gained in no other way.

As Sumner finished his rude lean-to, and placed the guns within its shelter for protection from the heavy night dews, Worth came up from the beach with his last load of drift-wood. It was now completely dark, and the notes of chuck-wills-widows were mingling with the "whoo,

A Story of the Everglades.

whoo, whoo ah-h!" of a great hoot owl in the forest behind them.

"Now for a fire and some supper," cried Sumner, cheerily. You've got some matches, haven't you?"

"I don't believe I have," replied Worth, anxiously feeling in his pockets. "I thought you must have some."

"No, I haven't a sign of one!" exclaimed Sumner, and an accent of hopelessness was for the first time allowed to enter his voice. "They are all aboard the canoes, and without a fire we are in a pretty pickle sure enough. I wonder how hungry we'll get before we make up our minds to eat raw duck? This is worse than losing the canoes. I declare I don't know what to do."

"Couldn't we somehow make a fire with a gun? Seems to me I have read of something of that kind," suggested Worth.

"Of course we can!" shouted Sumner, springing to his feet. "What a gump I was not to think of it! If we collect a lot of dry stuff and shoot into it, there is bound to be a spark or two that we can capture and coax into a flame."

So, with infinite pains, they felt around in the dark until they had collected a considerable pile of dry leaves, sticks, and other rubbish that they imagined would easily take fire. Then, throwing a loaded shell into a barrel of his gun, and placing the muzzle close to the collected kindlings, Sumner pulled the trigger. There was a blinding flash, a loud report that rolled far and wide through the heavy night air, and the heap of rubbish was blown into space. Not a leaf remained to show where it had been, and not the faintest spark relieved the darkness that instantly shut in more dense than ever.

"One cartridge spent in buying experience," remarked Sumner, as soon as he discovered the attempt to be a failure. "Now we'll try another. If you will kindly collect another pile of kindling, I'll prepare some fireworks on a different plan."

Thus saying, he spread his handkerchief on the ground, cut off the crimping of another shell with his pocket-knife, carefully extracted the shot and half the powder, and confined the remainder in the bottom of the shell with one of the wads. Then he moistened the powder that he had taken out, and rubbed it thoroughly into the handkerchief, which he placed in the second pile of sticks and leaves that Worth had by this time gathered. A shot taken at this with the lightly charged blank cartridge produced the desired effect. Five minutes later the cheerful blaze of a crackling fire illumined the scene, and banished a cloud of anxiety from the minds of the young castaways.

Chapter VIII.

LIFE ON THE LONELY ISLAND.

THE influence of a brisk wood-fire on a dark night is remarkable. Not only does it give freely of its heat and light, but gloom and despair are banished by its ruddy glow, while cheerfulness and hope spring forward as if by magic to occupy their vacant places. At least, this was the effect of the cheery blaze our canoemates had at length succeeded in coaxing into life, and though it had cost them two of their half-dozen cartridges, they felt that these had been well expended. Their prospects had looked dismal enough when they had been compelled to contemplate an existence without a fire; but with it to aid them, they felt equal to almost any emergency, and they turned to the preparing of their ducks for supper with renewed energy. Surely fire is well worthy of being classed with air and water as one of the things most necessary to human life and happiness.

Now that they had time to think of it, the boys were very hungry, for since an early breakfast they had eaten but a light lunch of crackers and jam. So they barely waited to assure themselves that their fire was going to burn, before the feathers from their ducks were flying in all directions. When the birds were plucked and cleaned, two sharpened sticks were thrust through their bodies. These were rested on one rock, with another above them to hold them in place, so that the ducks were lifted but a few inches above a great bed of glowing coals. Then the hungry lads sat down to watch them, and never, to their impatient belief, had two fowls taken so long to roast before. They began testing their condition by sticking the points of their knives into them long before there was a chance of their being done. At length Sumner declared that he was going to eat his even if it were still raw, and the half-cooked ducks were placed on two broad palm leaves that served at once as tables and plates.

"My! but isn't this fowl tough!" exclaimed Worth, as he struggled with his share of the feast. "Sole-leather and rubber are nothing to it."

"Yes," replied Sumner; "ten-ounce army duck would be easier eating than this fellow. I wish we could have stewed them with rice, a few bits of pork, a slice or two of onion, and a seasoning of pepper and salt. How do you think that would go?"

"Please don't mention such things," said Worth, working at a drumstick with teeth and both hands.

"Ducks ought always to be parboiled before roasting," remarked Sumner, wisely.

"I believe this fellow would be like eggs," replied Worth; "the more you boiled him the harder he would get."

However, hunger and young teeth can accomplish wonders, so it was not very long before two little heaps of cleanly-picked bones marked all that was left of the ducks, and though they could easily have eaten more, the boys wisely decided to reserve the doves for breakfast.

Although the darkness rendered it a difficult task, Sumner managed to cut a few armfuls more of palmetto leaves. These, shredded from their heavy stalks and spread thickly over the floor of the lean-to, made a couch decidedly more comfortable than a bed on the bare ground would have been.

They could do nothing more that night, and lying there in the firelight they had the first opportunity since discovering the loss of their canoes to thoroughly discuss the situation.

"What would our mothers say if they could

see us now, and know the fix we are in?" queried Worth, after a meditative silence.

"I'm awfully glad they can't know anything about it," replied Sumner.

"But I wish some one could know, so that they could send a boat for us. I am sure that we don't want to stay on this island for the rest of our lives."

"Of course not, and I don't propose to, even if no boat comes here."

"What do you propose to do?" inquired Worth, leaning on his elbow, and gazing at his companion with eager interest.

"Well, in the first place, I propose to explore this key thoroughly to-morrow, and see if any traces of the canoes are to be found, as well as what it will afford in the way of food and lumber. Then, if we don't find the canoes, and no boat comes along, I propose to build some kind of a raft, on which we can float over to Indian Key. While boats rarely pass this way, some are certain to pass within a short distance of it almost every day. So from there we would have little difficulty in getting taken off."

"Well," said Worth, regarding his companion admiringly, "I'm sure I couldn't build a raft with only a hatchet, and I'm awfully glad that I'm not here all alone. What can possibly have become of our canoes, anyway?"

"I'm sure I can't imagine," replied Sumner, "unless some one stole them, and I don't know of any one on the reef mean enough to do that. Besides, we haven't seen a sail all day, nor a sign of a human being. They couldn't have gone adrift, either — at least, I don't see how they could. So, on the whole, it's a conundrum that I give up. You'd better believe that I feel badly enough, though, over losing *Psyche*. That worries me a great deal more than how we are going to get away from here, for I never expect to own another such beauty as she is. But there's no use crying over what can't be helped, so let's go to sleep, and prepare for a fresh start to-morrow. Whenever you wake during the night you want to get up and throw a fresh stick on the fire, and I will do the same, for we can't afford to let it go out."

"All right," said Worth. "But, Sumner, there aren't any wild beasts or snakes on this key, are there?"

"I don't believe there are any snakes," was the reply, "while there certainly aren't any animals larger than 'coons, and they won't hurt any one. No, indeed, there is nothing to be afraid of here, and you may be as free from anxiety on that score as though you were in your own room in New York City. More so," he added, with a laugh; "for there you might have burglars, while here there is no chance of them. I only wish there was; for burglars in this part of the country would have to come in boats, and we might persuade them to take us off the key. Now go to sleep, old man, and pleasant dreams to you."

"Good-night," answered Worth, and closing his eyes, the boy made a resolute effort to sleep. Somehow he found it harder to do so now than it had been on his first night of camping out. The loss of the canoes seemed to have removed an element of safety on which he had depended, and to have suddenly placed him at an infinite distance beyond civilization, with all its protections. It was so awful to be imprisoned on this lonely isle, in those far-away southern seas. He wondered what his father and mother and Uncle Tracy were doing, and if there was a dance at the Ponce de Leon that night, and what his school-fellows in New York would say if they knew of his situation. He wondered and thought of these and a thousand other things, until finally he, too, fell asleep, and the silence of the lonely little camp was unbroken save by the voice of the great hoot owl, who called at regular intervals, "Whoo, whoo, whoo-ah!"

It still wanted an hour or so of moonrise, when

the waning firelight half disclosed a human figure that emerged from the woods behind the lean-to, and stealthily crouched in the black shadow beside it. For some moments it remained motionless, listening to the regular breathing of the boys. Then it moved noiselessly forward on hands and knees.

Suddenly Worth awoke, and sprang into a sitting posture. At the same time he uttered a startled cry, at the sound of which the creeping figure drew quickly back, and disappeared behind the trunk of a tree.

"What is it?" asked Sumner, who, awakened by Worth's cry, was also sitting up.

"I don't know," answered the boy, "but I am almost certain that some one was trying to pull my gun away."

Chapter IX.

THE NOCTURNAL VISITOR.

For a full minute the boys sat motionless, listening intently for any sound that should betray the presence of the intruder who, Worth was positive, had visited their camp. Once they both heard a slight rustling in the bushes behind them, and Worth, putting his hand on Sumner's arm, whispered, breathlessly,

"There!—hear that?"

"That's nothing," answered Sumner. "Probably that 'coon has come back to look for the rest of his supper."

"But a 'coon wouldn't pull at a gun," insisted Worth.

"Oh, you must have been dreaming," returned Sumner. "Your gun hasn't disappeared, has it?"

"No, but I am sure I felt it move. I threw my arm across it before I went to sleep, and its moving woke me. I felt it move once after I was awake, as though some one were trying to pull it away very gently. Then I sat up and

"SOME ONE WAS TRYING TO PULL MY GUN AWAY."

called out, 'Who's there?' but there wasn't any answer, and I didn't hear a sound. But, Sumner, there's some one on this island besides ourselves, I know there is, and he'll kill us if he gets the chance. Can't we get away somehow —can't we? I shall die of fright if we have to stay here any longer!"

"Yes, of course we can," answered Sumner, soothingly, "and we'll set about it as soon as daylight comes. Until then we'll keep a sharp lookout, though I can't believe there is a human being on the key besides ourselves. We surely would have seen some traces of him."

As the boy finished speaking he went outside and threw some more wood on the fire. In another minute a bright blaze had driven back the shadows from a wide circle about the little hut, and rendered it impossible for any one to approach without discovery. Then the canoemates sat with their precious guns in their hands, and talked in low tones until the moon rose above the trees behind them, flooding the whole scene with a light almost as bright as that of day.

By this time Worth's conversation began to grow unintelligible; his head sank lower and lower, until at length he slipped down from his sitting position fast asleep. Then Sumner thought he might as well lie down, and in another minute he, too, was in the land of dreams. Worth was very restless, and occasionally talked in his sleep, which is probably the reason why the dark form still crouching in the shadows behind the camp did not again venture to approach it.

It was broad daylight, and the sun was an hour high, when the boys next awoke, wondering whether their fright of the night before had been a reality or only a dream. Under the fear-dispelling influence of the sunlight even Worth was inclined to think it might have been the latter, while Sumner was sure of it.

After replenishing their fire, they went down to the beach in the hope of seeing a sail, and for their morning plunge in the clear water. There was nothing in sight; but while they were bathing, Sumner discovered a fine bunch of oysters. These, roasted in their shells, together with the birds saved from the evening before, made quite a satisfactory breakfast. After eating it, and carefully banking their fire with earth, they set forth to explore the island.

As they were most anxious to search for traces of the lost canoes, and had already penetrated the interior as far as the central pond of fresh-water, they decided to follow the coast-line as closely as possible. Accordingly, with their loaded guns over their shoulders, they set out along the water's edge. Their progress was slow, for in many places the mangroves were so thick that they found great difficulty in forcing a way through them. Then, too, they found a quantity of planks, many of which they hauled up, as well as they could, beyond the reach of the tide for future use. While thus engaged, the meridian sun and their appetites indicated the hour of noon before they reached a small grove of cocoanut-trees on the north end of the island, beneath which they decided to rest.

Sumner climbed one of the tall, smooth trunks, and cutting off a great bunch of nuts, in all stages of ripeness, let it fall to the ground with a crash. As he was about to descend, his eye was arrested by something that instantly occupied his earnest attention. It was only the stem of another bunch of nuts; but it had been cut, and that so recently that drops of fresh sap were still oozing from it. From his elevated perch he could also see where other bunches had been cut from trees near by, and he slid to the ground in a very reflective frame of mind. He could not bear, however, to arouse Worth's fears by communicating his suspicions until he had reduced them to a certainty. The nuts might have been taken by some passing sponger, though he did not believe they had been.

So he said nothing of his discovery while they lunched off of cocoanuts, ripe and partially so, and took refreshing draughts of their milk. He did, however, keep a sharp lookout, and finally spied what resembled a dim trail leading through the bushes behind them towards the interior.

Finally, on the pretext that he might get a shot at some doves, and asking Worth to remain where he was for a few minutes, Sumner entered the bushes, determined to discover the mystery, if that trail would lead him to it. He had not gone more than a hundred yards when his foot was caught by a low vine, and he plunged head first into a thick ty-ti bush. He fell with a great crash, and made such a noise in extricating himself from the thorny embrace that he did not hear a quick rush and a rustling of the undergrowth but a short distance from him. What he did hear, though, a minute after he regained his footing, was a startled cry, and the roar of Worth's gun. Then came a succession of yells, mingled with cries of murder, and such shouts for help, coupled with his own name, that for a moment he was paralyzed with bewilderment and a sickening fear. Then he bounded back down the dim trail, just in time to see Worth throw down his gun and rush towards the struggling figure of a negro. The latter was rolling on the ground

A Story of the Everglades.

at the foot of a cocoanut-tree, and uttering the most piercing yells.

As Worth became aware of Sumner's presence, he turned with a white, frightened face, exclaiming: "Oh, Sumner, what shall I do? I've killed him, and he is dying before my very eyes! Of course I didn't mean to, but he came on me so suddenly that I fired before I had time to think. The whole charge must have gone right through his body, judging from the agony he is in. What shall I do? Oh, what shall I do?"

"Well, he isn't dead yet, at all events," said Sumner. "Perhaps, if he will keep still for a minute and stop his yelling, we can find out where he is hurt and do something for him."

With this he attempted to catch hold of the struggling figure at his feet; but the negro rolled away from him, crying:

"Don't tech me, Marse Summer! Don't yo' tech me! I's shot full o' holes, an' I's gwine ter die. Oh Lordy! Oh Lordy! Sich pain as I's a-suff'rin'! An' I didn't kill nobody, nuther. I didn't nebber do no harm. An' now I's full ob holes. Oh Lordy! Oh Lordy!"

"Why, it's Quorum!" exclaimed Sumner, mentioning the name of one of the best cooks known to the Key West sponging fleet. Sumner had sailed with him, and knew him well. About a month before, the captain of the schooner on which he was employed had been found dead in his bunk. Quorum was accused of poisoning him for the sake of a sum of money that the captain was known to have had, but which could not now be found. The cook had been arrested, and an attempt was made to lynch him for the alleged crime. He had, however, succeeded in escaping, and had disappeared from the island. That no active search was made for him was because the money was found concealed in the captain's bunk, and it was proved that heart-disease was the cause of his death.

At length the negro, exhausted by his struggles, lay still, though groaning so heavily that Worth imagined him to be dying, and Sumner, bending over him, searched for the fatal wound. His face became more and more perplexed as the examination proceeded, until finally, in a vastly relieved tone, he exclaimed:

"You good-for-nothing old rascal! What do you mean by frightening us so? There isn't a scratch anywhere about you. Come, get up and explain yourself."

"Don't yo' trifle wif a ole man what's dyin', Marse Summer," said Quorum, interrupting his groans and sitting up.

"You are no more dying than I am," laughed

A Story of the Everglades.

Sumner, who was only too glad to be able to laugh after his recent anxiety. "I don't know what Worth, here, fired at, or what he hit; but it was certainly not you."

"Didn't I, really?" cried Worth. "Oh, I'm so glad! I don't know what possessed me to fire, anyhow; but when he came dashing out of the woods right towards me, my gun seemed to go off of its own accord."

"Yo' say I hain't hit nowheres, Marse Sumner?" asked the negro, doubtfully; "an' not eben hurted?"

"No," laughed Sumner, "not even 'hurted.' You know, Quorum, that I wouldn't hurt you for anything. I like your corn fritters and conch soup too much for that."

"Why for yo' a-huntin' de ole man, den?"

"Hunting you? We're not hunting you. What put such an idea into your head?"

"Kase ebberbody er huntin' him, an' er tryin' ter kill him for de murder what he nebber done."

"Of course you didn't do it. Captain Rube died of heart-disease. Everybody knows that now."

"What yo' say?" cried the negro, springing to his feet, his face radiant with joy. "He die ob he own sef, an' ebberybody know hit, an' dey hain't er huntin' ole Quorm any mo'? Glory be to de Lawd! Glory be to de Lawd! an' bress yo' honey face, Marse Summer, for de good news! De pore ole niggah been scare' 'mos' to def ebber sence he skip up de reef in a ole leaky skiff, what done got wrack on dis yer key. Now he free man, he hole he head up an' go cookin' agin. Bress de Lawd! Bress de Lawd!"

Chapter X.

WHOSE ARE THEY? AND WHERE DID THEY COME FROM?

"Look here," said Sumner, sternly, to the negro, after his excitement had somewhat subsided, "didn't you try to steal one of our guns last night?"

"Yes, honey, I's afeared I did," confessed the black man, humbly. "But I didn't know hit war you, Marse Summer, an' I did want er gun so powerful bad."

"I'm glad that mystery is cleared up, at any rate," said Worth, with a relieved air. "And I'm glad to find out that I was right about some one being in the camp, too. Now I wonder if he doesn't know something about our canoes?"

"Do you, Quorum, know anything about the canoes that we came here in?" asked Sumner.

"No, I don't know nuffin' 'bout no cooner. I's bin wonderin' what sort of er boat you'll come in, an' er lookin' fer him, but I don't see him nowhere."

"I suppose you would have stolen it if you had found it?"

"Maybe so, maybe so. Ole Quorm not 'sponsible fer what him do when he bein' hunted like er 'possum or er 'coon. Yo' like 'possum when he roasted, Marse Summer?"

"Indeed I do when you roast him, Quorum. Why? Have you got one?"

"Yes sah, cotch him in er trap dis berry mawnin'. I jist settin' hit agin when yo' come er trompin' troo de trees an' scare de pore ole niggah 'mos' to def. Now, if yo' say so, we go roas' him, and hab berry fine suppah."

"Certainly I say so. You lead the way, and we'll follow you. I tell you what, Worth, we've struck it rich in falling in with one of the best cooks on the reef."

"I don't know how I shall like 'possum," replied Worth, "for I have never eaten any; but I am sure it will make fully as good a meal as raw cocoanut. I do wish, though, that we had some bread, or at least some crackers, and a little butter."

"And sugar and coffee and bacon, and a cooking outfit," laughed Sumner. "I wouldn't mind spending a few days here if we had all those things."

"Wouldn't it be fine?" replied the boy, who had all his life revelled in luxuries that he hardly cared for, but would now have appreciated so highly the commonest of what are generally regarded as necessities.

As they talked in this strain, they followed the negro through the narrow trail leading back from the cocoanut grove to his camp. It was but a short distance from the place where Sumner had taken his header into the ty-ti bush. Here Quorum had built himself a snug palmetto hut in a place capitally concealed from observation, and had managed to surround himself with a number of rude comforts. A fire was smouldering in a rough stone fireplace, and from an adjoining limb hung the 'possum that they were to have for supper.

"Well," exclaimed Sumner, looking about him, "I don't see but what you are living like an African King, Quorum. Have you had plenty to eat since you came here?"

"Yes, sah. Plenty such as hit is—'possum, 'coon, turtle, fish, oyster, conch, cocoanut, banana, limes, lemons, an' paw-paw; but no terbakker. I tell yo', sah, dat a berry pore place what hab no terbakker."

"So you want tobacco to make you happy, and Worth wants bread and butter, and I want coffee. It seems that we all want something that we haven't got, and aren't likely to get in this world, doesn't it? But, Quorum, what on earth are you throwing all that iron into the fire for? It won't burn."

"No, him won't burn," answered the negro, chuckling at the idea, "but him good to bile de wattah."

As neither of the boys had the least idea what he meant, they watched him curiously. The iron that he had thrown into the fire, which he now heaped with wood, consisted of a number of old bolts that he had obtained from some wreckage on the beach. While these were heating, he filled a small hollow place in the rocks with water, and when the bolts were red-hot he dropped them into it. In about two seconds the water was boiling. Throwing a few handfuls of ashes into the boiling water, he soused the 'possum in it and held him there several minutes. After this he scraped the animal with a bit of iron hoop, and to the surprise of the boys, its hair came off almost without an effort. In a minute it was as bare as a suckling pig, which it greatly resembled. Shortly afterwards it was cleaned, washed, and ready for roasting.

Just here Sumner proposed that they return to their own camp, and do the roasting there, as from where they now were they had no chance of seeing any boats that might pass the island. As Quorum no longer felt the necessity for hid-

A Story of the Everglades. 77

ing, he readily agreed to this, and carrying with them the few articles belonging to him that were worth removing, they started through the woods towards what the boys already called home.

The afternoon was nearly spent when they entered the clearing and came in sight of their own little lean-to. Sumner, who was some distance in the lead, was the first to reach it. The others saw him suddenly stop, gaze at the hut as though fascinated by something inside of it, and then, without a word, start on a run towards the beach.

This curious action excited Worth's wonder; but when he reached the hut he did exactly the same thing. When Quorum, who came last, reached it, he gazed in open-eyed wonder, but did not move from the spot. A smile gradually overspread his face, and, with a long-drawn sigh of happy anticipation, he uttered the single word, "Terbakker."

"Do you see it?" asked Worth, breathlessly, as he joined Sumner on the beach.

"No; but perhaps it is behind the point. Let's go and take a look."

But when they reached the point there was no sign of the vessel that they fully expected to find there. More greatly puzzled than they had ever been before in all their lives, even at the mysterious disappearance of their canoes, the boys slowly retraced their steps towards the hut. It was completely filled with barrels, boxes, and various packages, most of which evidently contained provisions.

"There is a sack of coffee," remarked Sumner.

"And a box of crackers. And, yes, here is butter!" cried Worth, lifting the cover of a tin pail.

"Dat ar am sholy a box ob terbakker," put in Quorum, pointing to the unmistakable box, from which his eyes had not wandered since they first lit upon it.

"It certainly is," replied Sumner, in a voice expressive of the most unbounded amazement. "And there, if my eyes do not deceive me, are cases of milk, canned fruit, baked beans, and brown bread."

"Hams and bacon," added Worth.

"Kittles and pans," said Quorum.

"In fact," concluded Sumner, "there is a bountiful supply of provisions for several months, and a complete house-keeping outfit into the bargain. There is no doubt as to what these things are. The only unanswered questions are, Whom do they belong to, and how did they get here?"

"Perhaps whoever stole our canoes has left them here in part payment," suggested Worth.

A GREAT DISCOVERY.

"You might just as well say that Elijah's ravens had brought them," laughed Sumner.

"Marse Sumner, sah, 'scuse me, but do hit 'pear to yo' like hit would be stealin' to bang de kiver offen dat ar box, an' let de ole man hab jes one smell ob dat terbakker?" asked Quorum, humbly.

"No, Quorum, under the circumstances I don't believe it would," replied the boy, who forthwith proceeded to attack the box in question with his hatchet.

Chapter XI.

SUMNER DRIFTS AWAY ON A RAFT.

The display of layer upon layer of black plug tobacco such as Quorum had been accustomed to using for longer than he could remember caused the negro's eyes to glisten as though they saw so many ingots of pure gold. For more than two weeks he had longed unavailingly for a fragment of the precious weed. Now to have an unlimited quantity of it placed before him so very mysteriously and unexpectedly seemed to him the climax of everything most desirable and best worth living for. He sniffed at it eagerly, inhaling its fragrance with long, deep breaths. Then, producing a stubby black pipe from some hidden recess of his tattered clothing, he asked, pleadingly, for "jes one lilly smoke."

"After supper," said Sumner. "Get supper ready first, and then you shall smoke as much as you want to."

At this Quorum's countenance fell, and seating himself on the ground, he remarked, stubbornly: "No, sah. Ole Quor'm do no cookin' wifout him hab a smoke fust. No smoke, no cookin', no cookin', no suppah. Why yo' no gib one plug ob terbakker fur dat 'possum, eh? Him monstrous fine 'possum, but I willin' to sell him fur jes one lilly plug ob terbakker. Yo' can't buy him so cheap nowhar else, specially on dis yer oncibilized Niggly Wity Key."

"But it is not my tobacco," laughed Sumner, greatly amused at the old man's attitude and arguments.

"Who he b'long to, den?" demanded Quorum, quickly.

"I'm sure I don't know," answered the boy.

"Den he yourn. You fin' him. You keep him. Hit all de same like er wrack. Yo' catch him, nobody else want him, yo' keep him. Jes one lilly smoke, Marse Sumner—jes one; den de ole man go to cookin' de berry bestes yo' ebber seen. Come, Marse Sumner, jes one; dat's a honey-bug."

There was no resisting this pleading appeal, and cutting off enough for a single pipeful from one of the plugs, Sumner handed it to the negro, saying: "Well, then, if you must have it, take that, and hurry up with supper the very minute you have finished your smoke. I never was so hungry in my life, while Worth begins to look dangerously like a cannibal. Come, Worth, we must fly round, and build another palmetto shanty before dark. At this rate we'll have a town here before long."

Two hours of hard work found a second hut, much more pretentious than the first, nicely roofed in. By this time the sun was setting, and what was of infinitely more importance to the young canoemates, Quorum announced that supper was ready. And what a feast he had prepared! Had there ever been one half so good before? In the opinion of the boys, there certainly had not.

Quorum had felt no scruples about helping himself to the provisions so liberally provided, and if the boys had noticed what he was doing, they had not possessed the moral courage to interfere. As a result, he had baked the 'possum stuffed with cracker-crumbs, bits of pork and onions cut up fine, and well seasoned with salt and pepper, in a Dutch-oven. The oven had been set on a bed of coals, and a fire of light-wood knots built on its heavy iron lid. The 'possum had been surrounded with sweet-potatoes, and both were done to a brown crisp. Then there was coffee, with sugar and condensed milk, toasted hardtack with butter, and bananas for dessert.

"Talk about eating!" said Sumner.

"Or Delmonico's!" added Worth.

A Story of the Everglades. 83

As Quorum sat and watched them, a broad grin of happiness overspread his features, while wreaths of blue smoke curled gently upward above his woolly head. His pipe was again full, and he now had possession of an entire plug of tobacco, for which he felt profoundly grateful to some unknown benefactor.

Among other things in the hut, which the boys now called the storehouse, they had discovered a bale of blankets. These they did not hesitate to appropriate to their own use, and as they lay stretched on them, under their new roof, blinking sleepily at the fire, their comfort and happiness seemed almost to have attained perfection.

"Except for our canoes," said Sumner. "If we only had them, I, for one, should be perfectly happy; and to-morrow I am going to make preparations for finding them."

"How?" asked Worth; and for an hour or so they talked over their plans for the future. The intervals between their remarks became longer and longer, until finally, when Worth asked, "Whom do you suppose all those provisions belong to, anyway, Sumner?" the latter answered: "Give it up. I'm too sleepy to guess any more riddles to-night."

The boys slept almost without moving until

sunrise; but Quorum was frequently aroused to repel the invasions of certain 'coons that, but for his watchfulness, would have made free with the contents of the storehouse. He also had to protect the fire against a heavy shower that came on towards morning; and on each of these occasions he rewarded himself with a few whiffs of smoke from his black pipe.

The next morning the two boys, leaving Quorum to devise traps for the capture of the 'coons and prepare dinner, started out to collect some of the planks they had seen the day before. With these Sumner proposed to build a raft on which they could drift over to Indian Key with that afternoon's ebb-tide. Once there, he anticipated no difficulty in hailing some passing craft that could be chartered to search for their canoes, and carry them back to Key West in case the search proved fruitless.

As the channel from Lignum Vitæ, through which the strongest tide currents flowed, led directly past Indian Key and close to it, this plan seemed feasible. By noon the boys had towed around to the cove in front of their camp two heavy squared timbers and a number of boards. These they lashed together in the form of a rude raft. They had no nails, and but a limited supply of line for lashing, so that the raft was by no

GEORGE IS HAPPY.

means so strong as they could wish. Neither was it very buoyant, the material of which it was built being yellow pine, already somewhat water-soaked and floating very low. To their dismay, when it was completed, the boys found that instead of supporting three persons, as they hoped it would, it was awash and unsafe with but two of them on board.

"There's only one thing to be done," said Sumner, when this state of affairs became evident, "and that is for me to go alone. When I get hold of a craft of some kind, I can bring her here after you two; and if I don't find one, it will be an easy matter for me to come back on a flood-tide."

"But, Sumner, it seems awful for you to go 'way off there alone on such a crazy raft at this. Do you think it is absolutely necessary?"

"Yes," answered the other, whose mind was now intent only upon recovering his beautiful canoe, "I do think it is necessary for one of us to go. We can't stay here forever, living off of some unknown person's provisions. Besides, supposing those canoes should be wrecked and discovered in that condition, and the report that we were lost should reach Key West, how do you think our mothers would feel? Yes, indeed, it is necessary that I should go, and I mean to start the minute the tide serves."

Neither Worth nor Quorum could move Sumner from this determination, and it was with heavy hearts that they watched him, about four o'clock in the afternoon, step aboard the raft and shove out into the current, that had just begun to run ebb. He was provided with a long pole and a small box of provisions, the latter being placed in the middle of the raft.

Its movement was at first heavy and sluggish, but as soon as it felt the influence of the current, it was borne along with comparative speed. Thus a few minutes served to take the solitary voyager beyond earshot of his companions. For some time he could see them waving their hats, but at length their forms faded from his sight, and he realized that he was beyond reach of their assistance in case his undertaking should fail. Now that he could no longer note the speed with which he had left the island, his progress seemed irritatingly slow.

The channel was very crooked, and his clumsy craft frequently grounded on the projecting sand-bars at its many turns. In each case valuable time was lost in pushing it off and getting it again started. From this cause his rate of progress was so slow that Indian Key was still some distance ahead when the sun sank from sight in the western waters. Now, for the first time, Sumner experienced a feeling of uneasiness, and a doubt as to the success of his venture. He strove to add to the speed of his raft by poling, but as the depth of water was generally too great for him to touch bottom, nothing could be accomplished in that way.

Now he began to notice the numbers of sea-monsters that were going out with the tide and using his channel as their pathway to deeper waters. On all sides were to be seen the triangular fins of huge sharks rising above the surface so close to him that he could have touched them with his pole. He also saw hundreds of sawfish, stingarees, devil-fish with vampire-like wings, the vast bulks of ungainly jew-fish, porpoises, and other evil-looking creatures of great size and phenomenal activity. He shuddered to think what would be his fate if a slip or a misstep should precipitate him into the water among them. At length their forms were hidden from him by the darkness, and only their splashings and the gleaming trails of their progress through the phosphorescent water denoted their swarming presence.

Suddenly, while his attention was fixed upon these, he became aware that he was abreast of Indian Key and passing it. There was a shoal on the opposite side, and plunging his pole into it, he made a mighty effort to direct his raft towards land. All at once, without the slightest warning, the brittle pole snapped, and only by a violent effort did he save himself from plunging into the cruel waters.

Chapter XII.

PICKED UP IN THE GULF STREAM.

The snapping of that pole marked the bitterest moment of Sumner Rankin's life. With it went his only hope of navigating his rude craft to the friendly shore of the key, past which he now seemed to be drifting with terrible rapidity. He could make out the dim forms of its trees, and of the deserted buildings, in one of which he had proposed to spend the night. He could even hear the rustle of its palm leaves in the light evening breeze, and the gentle plash of waters on its rocky coast. It was so near that he could easily have swum to it. He thought of making the attempt, but a single glance at the phosphorescent flashes beneath him convinced him of its hopelessness. No, it was safer to remain where he was, even though he should be carried out to sea through one of the numerous channels in the outer reef. Supposing his raft should strand on the reef, what chance was there of its holding together until daylight, or even for a few minutes? He knew that if a sea should arise there was none.

Now Indian Key was lost to sight behind him, and he was alone, with only his own unhappy thoughts for company. He knew that those waters were seldom traversed by vessels of any description in the night-time, most of the reef sailors preferring to come to anchor at sunset. Above him shone the stars, and far ahead gleamed the white and red flashes of Alligator Light. All else was darkness and utter desolation.

The poor lad sat on the box containing his slender store of provisions, and buried his face in his hands. How thankful he was that his mother could not see him now! She was at least spared that sorrow. He wondered what she was doing. Then his thoughts turned to those whom he had left but a few hours before. Why had he not been content to stay with them, and await patiently the relief that must come to them sooner or later? Perhaps even now the mysterious owner of those goods had arrived, and Worth was sitting with a merry party beside the fire, while old Quorum was preparing supper. No, they must have already eaten supper, and now Quorum was blissfully smoking his pipe, while Worth was comfortably stretched out on his bed of blankets. Oh, what a fool he had been to let a false pride in his own strength and ability get the better of his prudence! He might have

A Story of the Everglades. 91

known that there were a hundred chances of being swept past the little rocky key to one of successfully landing on it. He had known it, but his obstinate pride in his own superior skill had not allowed him to acknowledge it, and now it was too late.

At length, feeling faint from hunger, the poor boy roused himself, and ate a few mouthfuls of food from his provision chest. As he contrasted this meal and its surroundings with the merry supper of the evening before, the wretchedness of his situation was forced upon him more strongly than ever. By this time a breeze that caused little waves to break upon and occasionally wash completely over the raft had sprung up in the south-west, and by the changing position of Alligator Light, Sumner became aware that he was drifting up the reef. The steadily increasing roar of its breakers informed him at the same time that he was approaching closer to it with each moment.

Finally he was abreast of the light, and a mile or so from it, while the sound of the breakers was all about him. He was on the line of the reef. In a few minutes more he would either have passed into the open sea beyond it, or his ill-built raft would strand and be broken to pieces on its cruel rocks. During the succeeding five minutes he almost held his breath. The strain of the suspense was awful, and the boy hardly knew which fate he dreaded the most. At the end of that time it was decided. The sound of the breakers certainly came from behind him. He had passed out through some channel, and was now on the open sea. At the same time the waves that washed over his raft were larger, so that before long he was thoroughly drenched by them, and sat shivering in the chill night wind. Now the strong current of the Gulf Stream aided the wind to bear him up the reef, and after a few hours the brightness of Alligator Light was so sensibly diminished that he knew he must be several miles from it.

Once during the night he saw the light of a steamship passing at no great distance from him; but his frantic cries for help were either unheard or unheeded, for no attention was paid to them. Then he began to pray for the daylight that seemed as though it would never come. How wearily the hours dragged and how cold he was! He was wet through, and chilled to the bone.

When at length the welcome dawn began to tinge the eastern sky, it found the lad half-lying on the raft, clinging to the lashings of the little provision chest, and lost to consciousness in the sleep of utter exhaustion. In this condition he was discovered by the keen-eyed lookout of a west-bound steamer that was hugging the reef to escape as much as might be the force of the Gulf Stream. With reversed engines and slackening speed, the great ship passed within a hundred yards of him, but he knew nothing of it.

Nor did he awake until he heard a gruff, but pitying voice close beside him, saying, "Poor fellow, he must be dead!" The next moment two pairs of powerful arms had dragged him into the boat that had been lowered for him, and as he sat up in its bottom rubbing his eyes, he seemed to have just awakened from a hideous nightmare. A few minutes later the boat with its crew had been hoisted to the deck, the steamer was again pursuing her way towards Key West, and Sumner, wrapped in hot blankets, was occupying a berth in a vacant stateroom, surrounded by the sympathizing faces of those who were anxious to anticipate his every want.

He was sound asleep when, half an hour from that time, the steamer neared Alligator Light, and a small boat was seen pulling off from it so as to intercept her. At the sight of this boat the first officer immediately began to collect such late papers and magazines as the passengers were willing to contribute, and tying them into a package. This he lashed to a bit of wood, which he intended to toss overboard for the light-keeper to pick up. In this way the reef lights are kept supplied with New York papers only three or four days old. The same papers, passing through the mails, do not reach the scattered dwellers on the keys for ten days or two weeks from the date of their publication.

As the steamer neared the boat from Alligator Light its occupant was seen to hold up a small package wrapped in canvas, which was at once understood to contain despatches that he wished to send to Key West. So the end of a light line was flung to him, he skilfully made the package fast to it without delaying the ship a moment, and it was hauled aboard. Among the letters that it contained was one directed to the editor of the only daily paper in Key West, and this was delivered promptly on the steamer's arrival at that port.

Late that afternoon, when Mrs. Rankin was slowly regaining her composure after the shock of Sumner's sudden and unlooked-for appearance at home, and was listening with breathless interest to an account of his recent adventures, a copy of the evening paper was left at the house. Sumner was too busy assuring his mother that

he was not suffering the slightest ill effect from his exposure of the night before, to look at it then. When, an hour later, he found time to do so, the leading item on the first page at once attracted his attention. It was headed, "A Mystery of the Reef," and after glancing hastily through it, the boy sprang to his feet, shouting:

"Hurrah, mother! The disappearance of the canoes is explained at last, and they are safe and sound, after all."

Chapter XIII.

A MYSTERY OF THE REEF.

As Mrs. Rankin came into the room, on hearing Sumner's exclamation, he read aloud the article in the daily *Equator* that had so excited him, and which was as follows:

"A MYSTERY OF THE REEF.

"By the steamship *Comal*, which arrived in this port to-day, we receive a curious bit of news from Keeper Spencer, of Alligator Light. On the evening of the 15th, as he was in the lantern of the tower preparing to light the lamp, he noticed two small craft of a most unusual description rapidly approaching from the direction of the keys. One appeared to be in tow of the other, but in neither could a human being be discovered. There were no signs of oars, sails, paddles, or steam, and yet the movement of the boats through the water was at the rate of about ten knots an hour. It was also very erratic, and though their general course was towards the

A Story of the Everglades.

reef, they approached it by a series of zigzags, now taking a sharp sheer to port, and directly another to starboard. As the keeper could not leave the tower at that moment, he directed Assistant Albury to take the light-house skiff, intercept the craft, if possible, and investigate their character.

With great difficulty, and after an exciting chase, Mr. Albury succeeded in getting alongside the leading boat of the two, and in making fast to it. It proved to be a decked canoe, of exquisite workmanship and fittings, completely equipped for cruising, bearing the name *Psyche* in silver letters on either bow. The second canoe, which was a counterpart of the first, was named *Cupid*. Both were in tow of an immense Jew-fish, which had succeeded in entangling itself in the cable with which the *Psyche* had evidently been anchored. It is probable that one of the flukes of the anchor caught in the creature's gills, though just how it happened will never be known, as Mr. Albury, being unable to capture the monster, was obliged to cut the cable and let him go. Nothing is known as to the fate of the owners of these canoes, and they are now at the light-house awaiting a claimant.

"Just as we go to press we learn that early this morning the *Comal* picked up a young man drifting in the Gulf, not far from Alligator Light. We were unable to obtain his name in time for insertion in to-day's paper, but will give it, with full particulars concerning him, in to-morrow's issue. He may be able to throw some light on the mystery of the canoes."

"I should rather think he could!" laughed Sumner, as he finished reading. "But did you ever hear of such a thing, mother? The idea of a rascally Jew-fish running off with our canoes! I never thought of such a thing as that happening. And how wonderfully it has all turned out! I should have looked everywhere for them rather than at Alligator Light. I should never have dared attempt to navigate the raft that far, either. To think, too, that I should have been picked up by the very steamer that brought the news! How dreadfully you would have felt on reading it, if I hadn't got here first! Wouldn't you, mother dear?"

"Indeed I should, my boy; and I shall never be able to express my gratitude for your wonderful preservation."

"But poor Worth!" exclaimed Sumner. "How I wish he knew all about it, and how awfully anxious he must be! I only hope he won't attempt to go to Indian Key to look for me before

I can get back there. That's something I must see about at once, and I must take the very first boat that goes up the reef. Just think how I should feel if anything were to happen to him, when Mr. Manton placed him in my care, too! If it wasn't for the way things have turned out, I should feel guilty at having left him there. I wouldn't have done it, though, if Quorum hadn't been on hand to look after him. He surely will keep him out of harm's way until I can get back."

"I hate to think of your going back there again," said Mrs. Rankin, with a sigh, "though of course it is your duty to do so. But you will be careful, and not run into any more such dreadful perils, won't you, dear?"

"Yes, mother; I promise not to run into a single peril that I can help, and if I meet one, I will try my best to get out of its way," laughed the boy, whose high spirits had quickly returned with the prospect of recovering his beloved canoe.

"Well," sighed Mrs. Rankin, "so long as you must go, I shouldn't be surprised if Lieutenant Carey would take you in the *Transit*. I believe he intends to leave to-morrow morning for a trip up the reef, and to make some kind of a survey in the Everglades. He has been staying here for a few days, and is up in his room now."

"Oh, mother!" cried the boy, springing to his feet, "the Everglades! How I should love to go!"

"Now, Sumner—" began Mrs. Rankin, in a tone of expostulation; but the boy had already left the room, and was on his way up-stairs.

Lieutenant Carey was an old friend, who had served under Commander Rankin, and had known Sumner ever since the boy was twelve years old. He had heard of his unexpected return, and only waited until the first interview between the young canoe-man and his mother should be ended before going down to greet him. Now he listened to Sumner's story with the deepest interest, and when it was ended, he said:

"Of course I will take you up the reef as far as Alligator, my boy, and shall be glad of your company. I only wish you would go with us as far as the main-land, and act as pilot through the Keys. They are not charted, you know, and as I have never been through them, I was on the point of engaging a fellow named Rust Norris as pilot, but I'd much rather have you. What do you say? Can't I enlist you in Uncle Sam's service for a week or so?"

"I should like nothing better," answered Sumner, "only, you see, I am bound just now to look after Worth Manton, and take him up the reef to Cape Florida, where we are due by the first of April."

"Perhaps we can persuade him to go along too. It won't be much out of your way, and you've lots of time to finish your trip between now and the first of April. I'll risk it anyhow, for I don't like the looks of that fellow Norris, and am only too glad of an excuse for not engaging him."

"Then there is Quorum, the cook," added Sumner, reflectively. "I wonder what will become of him?"

"A cook, do you say? What sort of a cook? A good one?"

"One of the best on the reef," replied Sumner.

"Then he is just the man I want to get hold of for our trip. I am only waiting now for a cook, and should start this evening if I had found one to suit me. If you will guarantee him, we'll get away at once, and make the old *Transit* hum up the reef in the hope of capturing him before he makes any other engagement."

"There is not much chance for him to make an engagement where he is now," laughed Sumner. "And, at any rate, I'm sure he wouldn't leave Worth until I get back. I shall be only too glad to start to-night though, for poor Worth must be terribly anxious, and the sooner I get to him the better."

Thus it was settled, and as soon as supper was over, after a loving, lingering farewell from his mother, who repeated over and over again her charges that he should shun all perilous adventures, the boy found himself once more afloat. Mrs. Rankin had promised to write a long letter to the Mantons that very evening, assuring them of Worth's safety up to the date of the day before, and being thus relieved from this duty, Sumner set forth, with a light heart on his second cruise up the reef.

The *Transit* was a comfortable, schooner-rigged sharpie, about sixty feet long, built by the Government for the use of the Coast Survey in shallow southern waters. She had great breadth of beam, and was a stanch sea-boat, though she drew but eighteen inches of water, and Lieutenant Carey had no hesitation in putting her outside for a night run up the Hawk Channel.

The especial duty now to be undertaken was an exploration of the Everglades to ascertain their value as a permanent reservation for the Florida Seminoles. These Indians, hemmed in on all sides by white settlers, were being gradually driven from one field and hunting-ground after another. In consequence they were becoming restive, and the necessity of doing something in the way of assuring them a permanent location had for some time been apparent. Thus a survey of the 'Glades was finally ordered, and Lieutenant Carey had been detailed for the duty, with permission to make up such a party to accompany him as he saw fit.

His present command on the *Transit* consisted of Ensign Sloe, and six men forward. It was intended that three of these should be taken into the 'Glades, while Mr. Sloe, with the other three, was to take the sharpie, from the point where the exploring party left her, around to Cape Florida, and there await their arrival.

On the deck of the schooner and towing behind her were three novel craft, in which Lieutenant Carey intended to conduct his explorations of the swamps and grassy waterways of the interior. One of these was an open basswood canoe built in Canada, shaped very much like a birch bark, and capable of carrying four men. The others were the odd-looking boats, with bottoms shaped like table-spoons, that are so popular as ducking-boats on the New Jersey coast, and are known as Barnegat cruisers. One of these was named *Terrapin* and the other *Gopher*, while the open canoe bore the Seminole name of *Hul-la-lah* (the wind).

Before a brisk southerly breeze, in spite of the boats dragging behind her, the *Transit* made rapid progress. Ere it was time to turn in, Key West Light was low in the water astern, while that on American Shoal shone steady and bright off the starboard bow. The wind held fresh all night, so that by morning both American Shoal and Sombrero had been passed, and the sharpie was off the western end of Lower Metacumba, with Alligator Light flashing out its last gleam in the light of the rising sun.

Chapter XIV.

WORTH AND QUORUM ARE MISSING.

As Sumner was anxious to reach Lignum Vitæ by the shortest possible route, the *Transit* was headed in through the channel between Lower Metacumba and Long keys. Both tide and wind being with her, the nimble-footed sharpie seemed to fly past the low reefs and sand-spits on either side. Now she skimmed by the feeding-grounds of flocks of gray pelicans, whose wise expressions and bald heads gave them the appearance of groups of old men, and then passed an old sponge crawl, or the worm-eaten hull of some ancient wreck, both of which were covered with countless numbers of cormorants, gannets, and gulls. Waiting, with outstretched necks and pinions half spread, until the schooner was within a stone's-throw, these would fly with discordant cries of anger, wheel in great circles, and return to the places from which they had been driven the moment the threatened danger had passed.

Even after the sharpie was well inside the bay,

and the island they sought was in sight, they could not lay a direct course towards it on account of a reef several miles in length that presented an effectual barrier to anything larger than a canoe. But one narrow channel cut through it, and this was away to the northward, close under a tiny mangrove key. Towards this then they steered, with Sumner at the tiller, for he was the only one on board familiar with the intricate navigation of those waters.

"You are certain that you are right, Sumner?" inquired Lieutenant Carey, anxiously, as they seemed about to drive headlong on the bar, and an ominous wake of muddy water showed that they were dragging bottom.

"Certain," answered the boy, quietly.

"All right, then; I've nothing to say."

Inch by inch the great centre-board rose in its trunk, and the slack of its pennant was taken in, as the water rapidly shoaled. Now she dragged so heavily that it seemed as though she were about to stop. Again the lieutenant looked at Sumner, and then cast a significant glance at the man stationed by the fore-sheet. But the boy never hesitated nor betrayed the least nervousness. An instant later the tiller was jammed hard over, there was a sharp order of "Trim in!" and, flying almost into the teeth of the wind, the light vessel shot through an opening so narrow that she scraped bottom on both sides, and in another moment was dashing through deep water on the opposite side of the bar.

From here the run to Lignum Vitæ was a long and short leg beat, with numerous shoals to be avoided. In spite of being kept busy with these, Sumner found time to note and wonder at a great column of smoke that rose from the island. What could Worth and Quorum be about? It looked as though they had managed to set the forest on fire. Filled with an uneasy apprehension, he jumped into a boat the moment the *Transit's* anchor was dropped in the well-remembered cove, and sculled himself ashore. To his amazement he heard the sound of many voices, and discovered a dozen or so of men hard at work apparently cutting down the forest and burning it.

As he stepped ashore, and looked in vain for the familiar figures of his friends, a pleasant-faced young man advanced from where the laborers were at work to meet him.

"Can you tell me, sir, what has become of a boy named Worth Manton and an old colored man whom I left here the day before yesterday?" Sumner inquired, anxiously.

"If you mean the two whom I found camped

here, and helping themselves to my provisions, I think I can," answered the young man, with a smile. "They went over to Indian Key last evening on the boat that brought me here yesterday. They were very anxious concerning the fate of a friend who left them the evening before, and went over there on a raft, I believe they said. Can it be that you are the person they are seeking?"

"Yes, sir, I am."

"Then you are Sumner Rankin, and I am very happy to meet you. My name is Haines. I have bought this key, and am clearing it, preparatory to having it planted with cocoanuts. The provisions and camp outfit that appeared here so mysteriously to you and your companions belong to me, and were left here by the mail-schooner on her way up the reef. I expected to arrive, with my men, about the same time, but was detained. I am very glad, however, that they came in time to relieve your distress. I am also much obliged to you for affording them a shelter from the rain, without which some of the things would have been injured. Now will you pardon my curiosity if I ask how you happen to arrive here in a schooner from that direction when your friends said you had gone the other way, and were confident of finding you on Indian Key?"

AS HE STEPPED ASHORE A PLEASANT-FACED YOUNG MAN ADVANCED TO MEET HIM.

A Story of the Everglades.

When Sumner had given a brief outline of his recent adventure, Mr. Haines said: "You certainly have had a most remarkable experience, and I am glad your friends did not know of it, for young Manton was worried enough about you as it was. However, you will soon rejoin them, and when you have recovered your canoes, if you feel so inclined, I should be pleased to have you return here as my guests for as long as you choose to stay."

Sumner thanked him, and said he should be happy to stop there on his return from the mainland. Then, begging to be excused, as he was impatient to go in search of his comrades, he jumped into his boat and returned to the *Transit*.

Lieutenant Carey was perfectly willing to proceed at once to Indian Key, but the tide was still running flood, and the breeze, which was each moment becoming lighter, was dead ahead for a run out through the channel. Under the circumstances, it would be useless to lift the anchor, and the impatient boy was forced to wait for the tide to turn. When it finally began to run ebb, the breeze had died out so entirely that there was not even the faintest ripple on the water, and another season of waiting was unavoidable.

By the lieutenant's invitation Mr. Haines came

off and dined with them. He proved a most charming companion, and laughed heartily at Sumner's description of the amazement with which he, Worth, and Quorum had discovered the mysterious godsend of provisions. Mr. Haines declared that it was one of the best jokes he had ever known; though he was in doubt as to whether it was on him or on them. He appreciated Sumner's impatience to be off, and when, late in the afternoon, a fair breeze sprang up, he made haste to take his leave that their departure might not be delayed.

It was nearly sunset when the *Transit* approached Indian Key so closely that objects the size of a man could be distinguished on it. Sumner was again at the helm, and he tried not to neglect his steering; but he could not keep his eyes from scanning anxiously every discernible foot of its surface. To his great disappointment not a soul appeared.

"They may be on the other side, keeping a lookout for passing vessels," suggested Lieutenant Carey.

Hoping that this might be the case, but still heavy-hearted and anxious, Sumner went ashore, accompanied by the lieutenant. For an hour they searched over every foot of the key, and through its deserted buildings, shouting as they went, but their search was in vain. Nothing was seen of the lost ones, nor had they left a trace to show that they had ever been on the island.

"It's no use," said Sumner at length; "they evidently are not here, and must have gone on in the boat that brought them when they failed to find me. Now, I don't know of anything to do but to go out to the light-house after the canoes, and then come back here and wait. If Worth has gone on up the reef, he must pass here on his way back, while if he has gone the other way, he will hear of me at Key West and come back here again. I'm awfully sorry that I can't go with you to the main-land, but I don't see how I possibly can under the circumstances."

Although the boy tried to speak cheerfully, and to take the brightest possible view of the disappearance of his young comrade, he was filled with anxiety, and it was with a heavy heart that he turned into his berth on board the schooner *Transit* that night.

Chapter XV.

WORTH AND QUORUM IN SEARCH OF SUMNER.

On the evening that Sumner left Worth and Quorum, and started on his adventurous voyage towards Indian Key, they watched him until distance and the approaching twilight hid him from their view. Quorum was the first to turn away and begin preparations for supper, while Worth still remained on the point straining his eyes towards the key, on which he fondly hoped that his friend was safely landed. At length it, too, disappeared in the gathering darkness, and he reluctantly turned his steps towards the camp. He was heavy-hearted, and had but little appetite for the bountiful supper that Quorum had so skilfully prepared. Noticing this, the old man tried to cheer him, saying:

"Don't yo' be so down in de mouf, Marse Worf. Dey hain't no 'casion fur worriment. I know Marse Summer Rankin fur a long time, an' I nebber know him in a fix yit what he don't slip outen, de same as er eel. I see him git in er plenty scrapes, but I don't see him git stuck. Him all right, and yo' no need to go er frettin' an' er mo'nin'. He be back ter-morrer bright an' smilin'. Now eat your suppah, honey, 'kase if yo' don't, ole Quor'm t'ink he cookin' no good."

In spite of the negro's consoling words, Worth's sleep that night was broken, and he started at every sound. Towards morning a crash and a smothered cry from the edge of the forest behind the camp caused him to start to his feet in alarm, and wake his companion. Although no further sound was heard, the boy was not satisfied until Quorum, taking a torch, discovered a thieving 'coon, caught and killed by the dead-fall that he had prepared for it. This was a simple figure **4** trap, set under a bit of board that was weighted with a heavy rock.

As soon as breakfast was over the next morning, Worth returned to his outlook station on the point, and remained there, with his eyes fixed on Indian Key, for several hours. It was nearly noon when he was startled by a shout from Quorum, who called out:

"Here him comin', honey! Here him comin' in er big schooner!"

Running back to the cove, which was not visible from where he had been sitting, Worth saw the schooner at which Quorum was gazing so eagerly. She was not more than a mile from them, and was bearing rapidly down towards the island, though from a direction opposite to that in which Indian Key lay. Still that did not dispel their hope that Sumner might be on board and coming to their relief. They could see that the schooner's deck was crowded with men, most of whom, as she approached more closely, proved to be negroes. Among them Worth's keen eyes distinguished, besides the whites composing her crew, one young white man who for a few minutes he was certain must be Sumner. As the schooner dropped anchor, and this person was sculled ashore in a small boat by one of the negroes, they saw, to their great disappointment, that he was a stranger.

He seemed surprised at seeing them on the key, and still more so when a glance at their camp showed the use they had been making of the stores they had so unexpectedly found there two days before.

"Oh, sir," exclaimed Worth, as the stranger landed, "have you seen anything of Sumner Rankin? I mean of a boy on a raft?"

"No, I have not," was the answer. "But I see that some one, and I expect it is the boy before me, has been making a free use of my stores."

"Are they yours?" asked Worth, flushing. "We

didn't know whose they were or who left them here, and as we were almost starving, we ventured to take what we needed; but I shall be glad to pay for whatever we have used." With this the boy produced a roll of bills, and looked inquiringly at the stranger.

"That's all right," laughed the other. "If you were starving, and had need of them, of course you acted rightly in taking them. I am only too glad that they were of use to you. I see, too, that you have sheltered them from the weather."

"Yes," replied Worth, "and it rained so hard night before last, that if they had not been under cover some of them would have been spoiled."

"Then we are quits," said the stranger; "and you have already more than paid for what you can have used in so short a time. I have bought this key, and intended to get here as soon as those things, which I sent up on the mail-boat, but was unexpectedly delayed. My name is Haines, and yours is—"

"Worth Manton," answered the boy; "and I was cruising up the reef in a canoe with my friend Sumner Rankin. When we got here, some one stole our canoes, or they got lost in some way, and so we were obliged to stay. We found this old negro Quorum here. Yesterday Sumner went over to Indian Key on a raft, to see if he could find the canoes, or get a vessel to take us off. We haven't seen anything of him since he left, and I am awfully afraid that something has happened to him."

"Oh, I guess not!" said the new-comer; "but if you like you can go over there on this schooner and look for him. The captain is in a great hurry to go on up the reef, as he is already two days late; but I guess he will drop you at the key, and stop there for you on his way back to Key West, if you want him to. But what is it that smells so good?" Here the speaker sniffed at an appetizing odor that was wafted to them from the direction of the little camp.

"I expect it is Quorum's 'coon that he is roasting for dinner," replied Worth.

"'Coon? That is something I have never tasted; but I should be most happy to experiment with it if it is half as good as it smells. Don't you want to invite me to dine with you?"

"Of course I do," laughed Worth; "especially as most of the dinner will consist of your own provisions."

A few minutes later they sat down to dinner together, and Mr. Haines declared it to be the best he had eaten since coming to that part of the country. He also praised the construction of the hut in which they ate, and thanked Worth for having provided him with such comfortable quarters.

While they were occupied with the meal, the black passengers of the schooner landed. Among them Quorum discovered friends who confirmed Sumner's statement that he was no longer suspected of the death of the sponging captain.

After dinner several hours were spent in landing the lumber and other freight with which the schooner was loaded. During this time Mr. Haines learned all the details of Worth's experience in canoeing up the reef, to which he listened with the greatest interest. He advised the boy to remain patiently where he was until Sumner's return, or at least until some word should be received from him. He was also anxious to engage the services of such a capital cook as Quorum had proved himself by the preparation of the dinner they had just eaten.

But the boy was so heart-sick with anxiety that he could not bear the thought of a further period of inaction, and Quorum declared he could not think of deserting the lad whom Sumner had left in his care.

So when the schooner was again ready to sail, they went on board, taking with them their guns and a supply of provisions with which Mr. Haines kindly provided them. He also insisted upon their taking a couple of blankets, which, he said, they could return whenever they had no further use for them, and he begged them to come back to the island in case they should be disappointed in their search. Thus they parted with an interchange of good wishes, and an hour later Worth and Quorum were set ashore on Indian Key. Although they had seen no sign of Sumner as they approached it, and the captain of the schooner had advised them to keep on with him up the reef, they could not make up their minds to do so until they had made a thorough examination of the key for traces of their lost comrade. Nor were they inclined to leave those parts so long as there was the faintest hope of hearing from him. So they were hurriedly set ashore, and the schooner continued on her way, the captain promising to stop there for them on his return trip.

Of course their search over the key was fruitless, and it was with heavy hearts that they made themselves comfortable for the night in one of its old buildings.

The next morning they wandered aimlessly over the narrow limits of the little island, or sat in the rickety porch of their house watching the column of smoke that, rising above Lignum Vitæ, marked the beginning of the cocoanut planter's operations. Turning from this, they would gaze longingly out to sea without knowing what they hoped to discover. Several schooners, bound both up and down the reef, passed during the morning, but none of them came within hailing distance of the key. At length Worth called out excitedly that he saw a canoe approaching from the direction of Alligator Light. At that distance the sail that he was watching certainly looked small enough to belong to a canoe; but as it came closer it grew larger, until it resolved itself into that of a good-sized cat-boat.

As it finally rounded to and came to anchor under the lee of the key, a man who was its sole occupant sculled ashore in a dingy containing several empty barrels. He was Assistant Keeper Albury, of Alligator Light, who had come to the key for a supply of water from its old cistern, the one belonging to the light having sprung a leak, and being nearly empty. He was surprised to find strangers on the key, and inquired at once what had become of their boat. After listening to their story and eager questions, he said:

"Well, if that doesn't beat all! No, we haven't seen anything out at the light of any young fellow floating on a raft; but we have got two canoes out there that answer pretty well the description of them you say you lost. What did you say their names were?"

"*Cupid* and *Psyche*," replied Worth.

"Then they are yours, for them's the very names. If you want to go out there with me after I fill my barrels, I've no doubt Mr. Spencer will give them up to you."

This they decided to do. So, after helping the man fill his water-barrels, they set sail with him for the light-house, which they reached late that afternoon, after some hours of tedious drifting in a calm.

A Story of the Everglades. 121

Chapter XVI.

A NIGHT IN ALLIGATOR LIGHT.

WHILE taking Worth and Quorum out to the light, Assistant Keeper Albury told them how the canoes had been towed out to sea by a Jew-fish, and described the difficulty he had had in capturing them. Although Worth listened to all this with interest, his pleasure in having the mystery cleared up, and at the prospect of recovering the canoes, was sadly dampened by his increasing anxiety concerning Sumner's fate. What can have become of him? was the question that he asked over and over again, but to which neither of the men could give an answer.

They were cordially welcomed to the light by the keeper, who was always glad to have visitors to his lonely domain, and Worth easily proved his ownership of the canoes by describing their contents.

The light-house was a skeleton frame-work of iron, with its lower platform about twelve feet above water that surrounded it on all sides. On this platform lay the two canoes, side by side, looking as fresh and unharmed as when Worth had last seen them at anchor off Lignum Vitæ. If Sumner had only been there, how he would have rejoiced over them! As it was, he gave them but a hurried examination to assure himself that they were all right, and then followed the keeper up the flight of iron steps leading to the house. The portion of this in which the men lived was a huge iron cylinder, surrounded by a balcony, and divided into several rooms. Above it rose a slender iron shaft, in which was a circular stairway leading to the lantern at its top. Worth ascended this with the keeper to witness the lighting of the great lamp, and the movements of the revolving machinery by which the red and white flashes were produced.

From this elevation a long line of keys was visible, while the one they had so recently left seemed quite close at hand. While gazing at it, Worth saw a schooner come down the channel from the direction of Lignum Vitæ, and lower her sails, as if for the night, under its lee.

"Oh, Mr. Spencer!" he cried, "there's a schooner come to anchor close to Indian Key. Perhaps her people are looking for us, and perhaps they have brought news of Sumner. Can't we take the canoes now and sail over there?"

"Bless you, no, lad! I wouldn't for anything have it on my conscience that I'd let you go sailing around these waters at night in those cockleshells. There's no doubt but what she'll stay there till morning, and if the weather is good, you can make a start as soon after daylight as ever you like; but you'll have to content yourself here till then. I couldn't think of letting you go before."

To this decision Worth was forced to submit, and after the lamp was lighted he followed the keeper to the living-rooms below. Here he found Quorum hard at work at his favorite occupation of cooking. He was preparing a most savory fish chowder, and when they sat down to supper both the keepers declared that in all their experience they had never tasted its equal. The second assistant keeper was then absent on the two-weeks' vacation, to which each of them was entitled after two months of service in the light. They only regretted that Quorum could not remain until his return, that he too might learn the possibilities of a fish chowder.

Worth was so charmed with his novel surroundings, and by the quaint bits of light-house experience related by the keepers, that until bedtime, he almost forgot his anxiety. When he had gone to bed in the scrupulously neat and clean guest-chamber, after charging the keepers to waken him at the earliest dawn, it returned in full force, and for a long time drove sleep from his eyes. As he lay listening to the keeper on watch making his half-hourly trips up to the lantern, and to the lapping of the waves about the iron piling of the foundation, he imagined all sorts of dreadful things as having happened to Sumner, and even after he fell asleep his dreams were of the same character.

From this unhappy dreaming he was awakened while it was still quite dark, though the keeper, who was standing beside his bed, assured him that day was breaking. At this, and remembering his cause for haste, the boy sprang out of bed and quickly dressed himself. In the outer room he found Quorum already up and waiting for him, and he also found a steaming pot of coffee. Fortified by a cup of this and a biscuit, he declared himself ready for the voyage back to Indian Key.

As they stepped outside, the light was sufficiently strong for them to dimly discern the distant line of keys, and preparations were at once made to place the canoes in the water. Worth's was the first swung from the platform davits and lowered, while he, descending a rope-ladder, one end of which touched the water, was ready to cast off the falls and step into her. Then Quorum was invited to do the same thing with the *Psyche;* but the old negro drew back apprehensively, exclaiming:

"No, sah, gen'l'men. De ole niggah am a big fool, but him no sich fool dat him t'ink hese'f er monkey, an' go climbin' down er rope wha' don' lead nowhar, 'cep' to er tickly egg-shell wha' done copsize de berry instink he tetch foot to um. No, sah, gen'l'men; ole Quor'm too smart fo' dat."

"Well, then, sit in the canoe where she is, and we'll lower you down in her."

To this plan the old man was finally induced to agree, and with great trepidation seated himself in the frail craft. The moment the men began to sway away on the falls, he would have jumped out if he could. As he was already swinging in mid-air, it was too late to do aught save remain where he was. Clutching the sides of the cockpit tightly with both hands, he closed up his eyes and resigned himself to his fate. His face assumed an ashen tinge, and his lips moved as though he were praying. He gave a convulsive start as the canoe dropped into the water, but he did not open his eyes nor relax his clutch of the coamings.

"Come, Quorum, get out your paddle. I'll show

you how to use it," shouted Worth, after he had cast off the falls.

But he might as well have addressed the lighthouse for all the notice the old man took of him. Finally, realizing that Quorum was utterly helpless, and incapable of action, from fright, Worth took the *Psyche* in tow, and paddling out from the light-house, bade the friendly keepers a cheery good-bye, and started on his laborious trip to Indian Key.

Although the sea was perfectly smooth, paddling two deeply laden canoes proved heavy work for one person, and Worth would have doubtless become exhausted long before reaching his destination had not a light breeze sprung up at sunrise. Aided by this, he made such good progress that in less than an hour he was rounding the point of Indian Key, behind which the *Transit* lay at anchor.

Sumner, who had just turned out, was gazing wistfully back at Lignum Vitæ, as though it still held the young comrade whose loss caused him to feel so depressed, when he started as though he had been shot, at the sound of his own name, uttered with a joyous shout but a short distance from him.

He could hardly credit his senses, or believe that he saw, sailing merrily towards him, the long-

QUORUM RESIGNS HIMSELF TO FATE.

lost canoes, bearing the very friends on whose account he had been so anxious but a moment before. At the same time Worth was equally bewildered and overcome with joyful emotions.

"Hurrah! Glory hallelujah!" shouted Sumner, in the fulness of rejoicing.

At this sound Quorum started as though from a trance, and opened his eyes for the first time since leaving the light. Whether he tumbled out of the canoe accidently or on purpose, no one, not even himself, ever found out; but the next instant he was in the water, puffing like a porpoise, and swimming towards the land. Fortunately the distance was short, so that in a few minutes he reached the rocks and pulled himself out on them. There, scrambling to his feet, and with the water pouring from him, he shook his fist at the craft he had so unceremoniously deserted, exclaiming:

"Dat's de fustes an' de lastes time ole Quor'm ebber go sailin' in er baby cradle! Yes, sah, de fustes an' de lastes!"

Chapter XVII.

AN ENTERTAINMENT ON THE KEY.

How Quorum managed to tumble out of the *Psyche* without upsetting her is a mystery, but he did it somehow. Seeing that he was easily making his way to the land, Worth continued on his course to the *Transit*, which he reached a minute later. The moment he stepped abroad, Sumner threw his arms about the boy with what was intended for a joyful hug. Worth returned it with interest. For a few seconds the two staggered about the deck in what looked decidedly like a wrestling match to the amused spectators of the scene, who had been attracted from below by Sumner's shout. Finally they tripped and rolled with a crash into the cockpit, where they scrambled to their feet, greeted by shouts of laughter from Lieutenant Carey and Ensign Sloe, while even the men forward were chuckling with ill-suppressed mirth.

Had Sumner and Worth been a few years older, they would probably have expressed their joy over this happy and unexpected meeting with a cordial hand-shake, and a few inquiries after each other's welfare during their separation. That would have been a man's way. Happily, all boys are not men, nor are their ways men's ways. Any genuine boy will understand that nothing short of a wrestling-match would have served to express the joy with which these two young hearts were relieved of the load of anxiety that had weighed so heavily upon them during the past three days.

"But how did you know the canoes were out at the light, Worth?" inquired Sumner, after the first boisterous greeting was over. "Excuse me! Let me introduce you to Lieutenant Carey and Ensign Sloe. And how did you get there? And how did you know that we were here?" exclaimed Sumner, in a breath, as soon as he had regained his feet.

"The keeper told us," answered Worth, shaking hands with those to whom he had just been introduced. "And I didn't know you were here. How did you get here, and what became of the raft? Did you ever see anything so absurd as Quorum? I don't believe he has opened his eyes since we left the light, and I actually thought he was turning white, he was so scared. Oh, Sumner, I never was so happy in my life!"

"Nor I," answered Sumner; "and if I ever

leave you again, you young scamp, before delivering you safe and sound to your lawful guardians, you'll know it."

"And you may be mighty sure I won't be left again," answered Worth. "No, siree! From this time on, you'll think I'm your shadow, I'll stick to you so close."

By this time Quorum had been brought aboard, and Sumner, shaking hands with him, gravely congratulated him upon having formed the habit of taking a plunge bath before breakfast. With a reproachful look at the lad, and without deigning to reply to his banter, Quorum turned away and dived into the little forward galley. Here he quickly made himself at home, and all the time he was drying by the galley stove he could be heard entertaining the colored cook of the *Transit* with a thrilling description of his recent voyage in "dat ar tickly nutshell. Mo' like er wash-basin dan er 'spectible boat; an' ef I don't hole her down wif bofe han's till dey done achin', she flop ober like er flapjack. I tell yo', chile, hit's er sperience sich as I don't want no mo' ob in all my sailin'.'"

Around the breakfast-table in the tiny aftersaloon, Sumner and Worth were comparing experiences and discussing their plans for the future.

"I tell you what it is, Sumner," exclaimed Worth, "I don't know about cruising any farther up this reef, where we are likely at any time to be seized and carried off to sea by some Jew-fish or other marine monster. Seems to me it's taking a big risk."

"Then why not come with us through the 'Glades?" laughed Lieutenant Carey. "There aren't any Jew-fish there. It will be almost the same as cruising on dry land all the way, and we'll bring you out at Cape Florida, the very point you are aiming for."

"I think that would be fine," answered Worth, who had no more idea of the nature of the Everglades than he had of the moon. "What do you say, Sumner?"

"It's the very thing I should most love to do," replied Sumner.

"Then you will go with us?" asked the Lieutenant.

"Yes, sir, we will," answered both the boys.

"Good! That settles it. Now do you suppose we can persuade your old darkey to go along as cook? I think you said he was a good one, Sumner?"

"Indeed he is!" exclaimed Worth; "the very best I ever knew. Oh yes, we must have Quorum along by all means."

When the plan was laid before him, Quorum shook his head doubtfully, and said:

"I allus hear dem Ebberglades is a ter'ble place. Dey's full ob lions an' tigers, sayin' nuffin' ob wild Injuns an' cannon-balls" (probably Quorum meant cannibals). "But ef dem two chilluns boun' ter go, I spec' ole Quor'm hab ter go 'long ter look after um, an' see dat dey's kep' outen danger. Hit's er mighty owdacious undertaking fer de ole man; but dish yere er peart-looking wessel, an' maybe she take us troo all right."

"But we are not going in this vessel," laughed Sumner. "We couldn't take her through the 'Glades."

"How yo go, den?" asked the negro, looking up quickly. "Not in them tickly li'l' cooners?"

"Yes, some of us will go in the canoes, but you will have a much larger boat; one that you can't possibly upset."

"When I see him, den I tell yo' ef I er gwine." And this was the only promise that Quorum could be induced to give.

"Very well," said Lieutenant Carey, when this was reported to him; "we will rig up the cruisers, and let Quorum sail one of them in to Lignum Vitæ. One of the men shall take the other, you two will sail your own canoes, and I will sail mine, while Mr. Sloc shall follow with the *Transit*. When Mr. Haines sees us coming he'll think he is looking at a regatta of the Reef Yacht Club."

This plan suited the boys perfectly, and the next two hours were spent in getting all the boats into the water, overhauling sails, spars, etc. When Quorum saw the Barnegat cruiser that was assigned to him, he declared, "Hit done look like er punkin seed, an' I don't beliebe hit fit fer sailin' nohow." It was only with the greatest difficulty that he could be persuaded to try the strange-looking craft. When he finally did so, his eyes opened wide with astonishment at her speed and stiffness, and the ease with which she was handled.

Each of the cruisers carried a large sprit-sail, and was fitted with a pair of oars. They were provided with centre-boards, were fair sailers, easy to row, practically non-capsizable, and capable of carrying heavy loads without materially increasing their draught.

Quorum was a good sailor, and as soon as he became somewhat accustomed to his craft he began to handle her in a way that showed an appreciation of her qualities. When he shot ahead, after a little brush with the other cruiser, the *Melon Seed*—as he termed her—his black face fairly beamed with delight.

"Your man is as tickled with that boat as a

child with a new toy," remarked Lieutenant Carey to Sumner, "and I guess there is no doubt now but what he will go with us."

The Lieutenant's open paddling canoe was fitted with a leg-of-mutton sail, but no centre-board. Thus the sail was only available for running before the wind, which on this occasion happened to be fair. The three canoes and the two cruisers, starting on their race to Lignum Vitæ, formed a very pretty sight. As they were followed by the *Transit*, and by the schooner that had carried Worth and Quorum to Indian Key, which came along on her return trip just then, it is no wonder that Mr. Haines regarded the approaching fleet with astonishment.

The race was won by Sumner in the *Psyche*, with Quorum in his *Punkin Seed*, and wildly excited, close behind. The other three were well bunched, and the two schooners were worked under foresails only, to keep from running them down.

All hands were made heartily welcome by the proprietor of Lignum Vitæ, who was made happy by the information that they proposed to stay there that night. On hearing this he immediately began to plan a grand dinner to which everybody was invited, and an entertainment for the evening. He and Lieutenant Carey spent the afternoon in arranging for the entertainment, the four cooks, with Quorum at their head, spent it in preparing a most elaborate dinner, and the others spent it fishing and sailing match-races between the various small boats. As the hours flew busily and happily by, Sumner and Worth wondered how they could ever have felt wretched and forlorn in such a pleasant place.

The dinner, which was served shortly before sunset, was a veritable feast. On its bill of fare appeared oysters, green-turtle soup, fish chowder, turtle steaks, baked kingfish, stewed ducks, roasted 'possum, a variety of canned vegetables, an immense plum duff, canned fruits, crackers, cheese, and coffee; while the whole was seasoned with the sauce of hearty appetites and capital digestions. It was a substantial meal, as well as a merry one, and it gave Worth Manton a new insight into the possibilities of life on the Florida Keys.

By hard work Mr. Haines had succeeded in raising the frame of the little one-story house that he intended to occupy, and in getting the floor laid. This was to be the scene of the entertainment, and an hour or so after dinner all hands were collected here. Several large bonfires shed a cheerful light on the circle of expectant faces, and cast wavering shadows over the platform.

The first number on the programme was an overture by the Lignum Vitæ Band, which consisted of Mr. Haines's banjo, Lieutenant Carey's guitar, Ensign Sloe's violin, and a flute played by one of the *Transit's* men. Then Worth danced a clog, and was received with immense applause. He was followed by Sumner, who performed a number of sleight-of-hand tricks that drew forth exclamations of astonishment from the negroes. A mouth-organ quartet by four of the negro hands, was followed by Mr. Haines's banjo solo. This was of such an inspiring character that all the negroes patted time to it, and finally Quorum sprang upon the platform and, with his beloved pipe still held tightly between his teeth, began to shuffle a breakdown in such a comical manner that it was received with tumultuous applause and roars of laughter. Solo and chorus singing followed, and the entertainment wound up with the singing of "Annie Laurie" by a quartet of sailors.

Both Sumner and Worth were certain that they had never passed a more enjoyable evening, and were almost sorry that they had promised to leave there and start for the Everglades on the following morning.

QUORUM DANCES A BREAK-DOWN.

Chapter XVIII.

OFF FOR THE EVERGLADES.

Both Sumner and Worth were by this time quite used to being turned out of bed while it was still dark, and told that it was morning and time to make a start. So, when the familiar summons was heard, a few hours after their evening of fun, they obeyed them, though not without some sleepy grumblings and protests. The stars were still shining when they went on deck for a look at the weather, and they shivered with the chill of the damp night air.

There were faint evidences of daylight, however, and the welcome fragrance of coffee was issuing from the galley. They felt better after drinking a cup of it, but did not consider themselves fairly awake until the sails were hoisted, the anchor lifted, and the *Transit* began to move slowly out from under Lignum Vitæ.

Just as they were getting fairly under way, a sleepy hail of " Good-bye, and good-luck to you !" came from the edge of the forest on the key where the night shadows still lingered. Then, with answering shouts of "Good-bye, Mr. Haines! Good-bye to Lignum Vitæ!" they were off.

The reason for such an early start was that, with four boats in tow, even the *Transit* could not be expected to make very good speed, and Mr. Carey was anxious to cover the sixty-mile run to Cape Sable before dark.

For the first three hours Sumner was kept constantly at the helm, directing the course of the schooner through a multiplicity of tortuous channels, between coral-reefs, oyster-bars, and a score of low-lying mangrove keys. All this time Lieutenant Carey stood beside him, keeping track of the courses steered and noting on his chart the position of the channels, together with the names of· the keys, so far as Sumner was able to give them. The knowledge that the lad displayed of these uncharted waters, and the skill with which he handled the schooner, so excited the lieutenant's admiration that he finally said: "I declare, Sumner, I don't believe there is a better pilot in the whole Key West sponging-fleet than you! How on earth do you remember it all?"

"I don't know," laughed Sumner, "I expect it comes natural, as the man said when asked what made him so lazy."

"Well," said the lieutenant, "I am mighty glad to have you along instead of that fellow

Rust Norris, though he did intimate that your ignorance of the reef would get us into trouble. He was greatly cut up when I told him that, as you were going with me, I should not require his services, and tried to say some mean things about you; but I shut him up very quickly. He doesn't seem to be a friend of yours, though."

"I don't know why he shouldn't be," replied Sumner, "I am sure I feel friendly enough towards him. I suppose it must be because I wouldn't let him try my canoe the other day, and left him on the buoy that night. I only meant that as a joke though, and was just about to start out for him, when I saw a fisherman pick him up."

Here Sumner related the incident referred to, and the lieutenant said, as Mr. Manton had, that the fellow was rightly served. Then the subject was dropped, and they thought of it no more.

As they were now in open water, with all traces of land rapidly fading in the distance behind them, Sumner laid a course for Sandy Key, the only one they would see before reaching Cape Sable, resigned the tiller, and invited Worth to try his hand at trolling. The *Transit* being well provided with fishing tackle they soon had two long trolling lines towing astern. Worth said he was going in for big fish, and so attached to the end of his line a bright leaden squid terminating in a heavy, finely-tempered hook.

Sumner, believing that there would be as much sport and more profit in trying for those that were smaller, but more plentiful, used a much lighter hook, baited with a bit of white rag. Worth would not believe that any fish could be so foolish as to bite at such a bait. His incredulity quickly vanished, however, as Sumner began to pull in, almost as fast as he could throw his line overboard, numbers of Crevallé, or "Jack," beautiful fellows tinted with amber, silver, and blue, and Spanish mackerel, one of the finest fish in southern waters. Seeing that Sumner was having all the fun, while he could not get a bite, Worth began to haul in his line with a view to putting on a smaller hook, and baiting it with a bit of rag. Suddenly there was a swish through the water, a bar of silver gleamed for an instant in the air, a hundred feet astern, and Worth's line began to whiz through his hands with lightning-like rapidity. With a howl of pain, he dropped it as though it had been a red-hot coal, and began dancing about the cockpit, wringing his hands and blowing his fingers.

"Snub him, Worth, quick! or he'll have your line," cried Sumner, springing to his friend's assistance. "It's a barracuda, and a big one!"

He got a turn around the rudder-post just in time to save the line, and then began a fight that set the young fisherman's blood to tingling with excitement. In spite of his smarting fingers, Worth insisted upon pulling in his own fish; while the barracuda seemed equally intent upon pulling his captor overboard. Such leaping and splashing, such vicious tugs and wild rushes ahead, astern, and off to one side, as that barracuda made, were far beyond anything in the way of fishing that Worth had ever experienced. For ten minutes the fight was maintained with equal vigor on both sides. Every inch of slack was carefully taken in. With the stout rudder-post to aid him, Worth was slowly but surely gaining the victory, and the great, steely-blue fish was drawn closer and closer to the schooner.

At length he was within fifty feet, and Worth's flushed face was lighting with triumph, when, all at once there came a rush of some vast, white object astern. A huge pair of open jaws, lined with glistening rows of teeth, closed with a vicious snap, and a moment later Worth, whose face was a picture of bewildered amazement, pulled in the head of his fish minus its body.

"Was it a whale, do you think?" he asked, soberly, turning to Sumner.

"No," replied the other, laughing at his companion's crestfallen appearance, " but it was the biggest kind of a shark, and he would have snapped you in two as easily as he did that barracuda, if you had been at that end of the line."

By noon they had left Sandy Key astern, and before sunset they had passed the stately cocoanut groves on Cape Sable and Palm Point, and were rounding Northwest Cape. Just at dusk they headed into a creek, not more than twenty feet wide, and directly afterwards came to anchor in the deep, roomy basin to which it was the entrance. The basin was already occupied by a small sloop, and as Sumner's knowledge of those waters did not extend beyond that point, Lieutenant Cary anticipated being able to gain some information from her crew. With this in view he anchored but a short distance from her, and after everything was made snug for the night, he hailed her with:

"Hello on board the sloop!"

"Hello yourself! What schooner is that?"

"The Government schooner *Transit*, and I should be very glad to see any of you on board."

"Where are you bound?"

"Into the 'Glades. Will you come over after a while, or shall I go aboard the sloop? I want to have a talk with you."

"I reckon we'll come over."

A Story of the Everglades. 143

"Those fellows don't seem inclined to be very sociable," remarked the Lieutenant to Ensign Sloe, as they went down into the cabin to supper. At the same time Sumner was saying to Worth, "I wonder who that fellow is? His voice sounded very familiar."

When they again came on deck after supper, the night was so dark that they could not see the sloop, though they supposed her to be lying close to them.

"Hello aboard the sloop!" again hailed Lieutenant Carey.

There was no answer, nor did several hails serve to bring a reply of any kind.

"Let's take my canoe and go for a look at those fellows, Sumner," said the Lieutenant. "They have quite excited my curiosity."

In a few minutes the canoe was afloat, and its occupants were paddling in the direction of where the sloop was thought to lie. For half an hour they paddled back and forth, and in circles, being guided in their movements by the bright riding light of the *Transit*. Once they struck a floating oar that seemed to be attached to a cable; but they could discover no trace of the sloop, nor did their repeated hailings bring forth a single answer.

At length, greatly perplexed by such unaccountable behavior on the part of the sloop's crew, and nearly devoured by the clouds of mosquitoes that swarmed above the lagoon, they returned to the schooner, and thankfully sought the shelter of her wire-screened cabin.

Chapter XIX.

THE CANOES ARE AGAIN LOST, AND AGAIN FOUND.

In that snug harbor there was so little chance of danger that no watch was kept, and all hands turning in, after a pleasant evening spent in smoking and discussing plans, slept soundly until morning. Although the sun had gone down in a blaze of ominous glory the evening before, and the breeze had died out in an absolute calm, no one was fully prepared for the wonderful change of scene disclosed by the morning. While their land-locked harbor was still as placid as a millpond where they were anchored, it was blackened and roughened by the gusts of fierce squalls but a short distance from them. The continuous roar of breakers outside denoted a furious sea, the cause of which was shown by the lashing tree-tops and the howlings of a gale overhead. The sky was hidden behind masses of whirling clouds, while after the tropical weather to which they had become accustomed, the air seemed very cold, though the mercury had not fallen below 50°. The gale was a typical Norther, that, sweeping down from Texas prairies, had gathered strength in its unchecked progress across the Gulf, and was now hurling itself with furious energy against the low Florida coast.

"Whew! What a day!" cried Sumner, as he emerged from the warm cabin and stood shivering in the cockpit. "I tell you what, old man, I'm glad we are in this snug haven, instead of outside."

"So am I," said Worth, who had followed Sumner, and to whom these remarks were addressed. "I'm afraid canoes would stand a pretty sorry chance out there just now."

"Canoes! Well, I should say so! They'd be— Great Scott! Where *are* the canoes and the cruisers?"

Sumner had just taken his first glance astern, and as he uttered this exclamation he sprang to the little after-deck, and stared about him. The three canoes and the two cruisers had been left for the night attached to a single stout line which was made fast to the *Transit's* rudder-post. Now they were gone, and not a sign of them was to be seen as far as the eye could reach.

"If that doesn't beat anything I ever heard of!" exclaimed Sumner, in bewilderment.

"I should think a jew-fish big enough to take

A Story of the Everglades. 147

them all might just as well have taken the schooner, too," said Worth.

"Yes, I expect she will be stolen from under us the next thing we know," replied Sumner, "and I expect if we ever get our canoes again we'd better put them into a burglar-proof safe and hire a man with a dog to watch them nights. I never heard of anybody losing canoes as easily as we do. Where do you suppose they can have gone to, sir?"

This question was addressed to Lieutenant Carey, who, together with Ensign Sloe, had been attracted to the deck by Sumner's first dismayed exclamation.

"I've no more idea than you have," replied the Lieutenant, gravely. "The jew-fish is not to blame this time, at any rate, for there was no anchor down that he could get hold of, and this rope has evidently been cut." Here the speaker displayed the end of the rope that had hung over the stern, and pointed to the clean cut by which it had been severed. "It is evident that some human agency has been at work," he continued, "and I am inclined to connect it with the strange behavior of the fellows on that sloop; though what their object in stealing our boats was, I can't imagine. It is a very serious matter to us, however, and one that calls for prompt investigation. As this wind must have sprung up early in the night, it is hardly probable that the boats can have been taken out to sea, and if they were not they must be somewhere in this lagoon, perhaps concealed in the mangroves, or in one of the sloughs that empty into it. It is lucky that we have the canvas boat left, for I should hate to try and navigate the *Transit* in these unknown waters with such a gale blowing."

The canvas boat, of which the Lieutenant spoke, was a folding affair that was stowed under the cockpit floor, and was a part of the schooner's regular outfit. Although it was very light, it could easily accommodate three persons, and was a capital thing to fall back on in an emergency like the present.

Mr. Carey ordered it to be got out and put in shape at once. After breakfast he and Sumner, with one of the crew to row, stepped into it and started on their search. They skirted the shore as closely as possible, both to escape the force of the wind, and that they might the more carefully examine the dense mangrove thickets that, with occasional stretches of white beach, formed the coast-line.

The mangrove, which here attains the size of oaks, is one of the most curious of trees, and in one particular closely resembles the banyan. Its small yellow blossom, which is eagerly sought by honey-bees, forms a long brown seed about the size and shape of a cigar. This, falling off, readily takes root in mud-flats, beneath shallow salt or brackish water, and shoots up a straight slender stem having numerous branches. Some of these branches bend downward to the water, sending their tips into the mud, where they in turn take root. At length the tree is thus surrounded by a circle of woody arches that soon become strong enough to support the weight of a man. As the tree increases in height, the upper branches send down long straight shoots that also take root and form independent trunks. Mangroves grow with marvellous rapidity, and quickly cover large areas, where their thickly interlaced, arching roots hold all manner of drift and sea-weed, until finally a soil is formed in which the seeds of coarse grasses and other vegetation sprout and flourish. Thus, in the course of time, an island of dry land appears and is lifted above the water. In this way the coral reefs of the Florida coast are gradually transformed into verdant keys, the mangrove taking up and continuing the work of island building just below the surface of the water, where the coral insect leaves off. The mangrove is covered with a thick foliage of small glossy leaves, that is such a favorite haunt for mosquitoes, that wherever mangroves grow, mosquitoes are found in countless millions.

Skirting this wonderful mangrove forest, and occasionally penetrating shallow bayous in which herons, cranes, ibises, pelicans, and curlews swam and waded, the occupants of the canvas boat searched for several hours in vain. Finally, as they were on the opposite side of the broad lagoon from their starting-point, and exposed to the full force of the wind, Sumner called out that he saw something that looked like masts on the edge of a distant clump of mangroves. It was no easy task to navigate successfully through the heavy sea running at this point; but when they had accomplished it, they were rewarded by seeing the entire missing fleet piled up in the greatest confusion among the mangroves, which at this place extended far out into the water. Before they reached them both the Lieutenant and Sumner were obliged to jump overboard in water above their waists, to prevent the canvas boat from swamping in the breakers.

The picture presented by their stranded fleet looked like one of utter ruin. Sumner trembled for the fate of his precious canoe, and the Lieutenant wondered if his expedition had thus been brought to an untimely end. There was a small beach but a short distance away, to which the sailor took the canvas boat, and then returned to help them clear the wrecks. One by one the several craft, all of them full of water, were extricated from the tangled mass, and dragged to the beach for examination. The three canoes were found to be badly scratched, and damaged so far as looks went; but still sound and seaworthy. This was undoubtedly owing to their lightness, and the exceeding care with which canoes are built. In their construction the question of expense is not considered; consequently, being built of the best material, by the most skilful workmen, they are stronger than ordinary craft many times their size.

Their sails were muddied and torn, and some of their slender spars were broken; but as most of their cargoes had been transferred to the *Transit* before leaving Lignum Vitæ, this was the extent of their injury. Sumner was jubilant when a careful examination of every part of them revealed this fact; but Mr. Carey, who was devoting his attention to the cruisers, looked very grave. Both of them were badly stove, and it was evident that only extensive repairs could render them again fit for service.

"Who could have done this thing, and why was it done?" he repeated over and over again in deep perplexity; while Sumner, equally at fault, tried to recall whose voice it was that had seemed so familiar when they had exchanged hails with the sloop.

After emptying the canoes, and hauling the cruisers high up on the beach, where they were to be left for the present, the party set forth on their return trip. The Lieutenant went in his own canoe, Sumner in his, while the sailor in the canvas boat towed the *Cupid.*

As they neared the schooner they saw her people pointing eagerly towards a bit of beach near the head of the creek through which they had entered the lagoon the evening before. Looking in that direction, they saw a white man beckoning to them and shouting, though they could not distinguish his words.

Readily understanding that he was in distress of some kind, the Lieutenant and Sumner headed their canoes in his direction. As they neared him, they saw that he was hatless, and clad only in a shirt and trousers that were torn and water-soaked. The first words they could distinguish were:

"Our boat is going to pieces outside, and Rust Norris is in her with a broken arm."

"Rust Norris!" That was the name Sumner had been racking his memory for, and his was the voice that had come to them from the sloop on the preceding evening.

A Story of the Everglades. 153

Chapter XX.

THE *PSYCHE* AS A LIFE-BOAT.

"Just where does the sloop lie?" asked Sumner, as the bow of his canoe ran on to the beach where the man stood.

The latter explained the position of the stranded vessel so clearly that the boy, who was familiar with the locality, comprehended it in a moment.

"She's about a mile from the mouth of the creek, and a quarter off shore," said the man. "When the tide went down I partly swum and partly waded to the beach. I don't know how I ever got ashore alive, but the thought of poor Rust out there kinder nerved me on, and so I made it at last. I wouldn't do it again, though, for all the money in Key West. Now I've been here so long waiting for help, and the tide's rising again so fast, that I'm afraid it's all day with poor Rust. If he ain't swept off the wrack by this time he soon will be, and I don't know as there is anything can be done for him. It wouldn't be possible for the schooner to get anywhere near the wrack, she's dragged in so fur over the reefs, and the small boat isn't built that could live in them seas."

"Yes, she is," said Sumner, quietly, but with a very pale face; "this boat that I am sitting in can live out there, and she's got to do it, too." So saying, he set his double-bladed paddle into the sand, and with a vigorous shove sent the light craft gliding backward into deep water.

The man stared at him in speechless amazement, while the Lieutenant called out: "Don't try it, Sumner! You must be crazy to think of such a thing! You'll only be throwing away your own life for nothing! Come back, and we'll think of some other plan."

"There isn't time to think of another plan," Sumner called back over his shoulder. "I must go, and I know I can do it. If you will have some of the men out there on the beach, ready to help us land, we'll make it easy enough. Good-bye!"

Impelled by vigorous strokes of Sumner's paddle, the *Psyche* was already gliding down the smooth waters of the sheltered creek, and it was too late to restrain the impetuous young canoeman from carrying out his project. Realizing this, and also that Sumner's plan, hazardous as it seemed, was the only feasible one, Lieutenant

A Story of the Everglades. 155

Carey, with a heavy heart, set about doing his own share of the work in hand. He took the stranger off to the schooner, and after swallowing a cup of hot coffee, of which he stood greatly in need, the man declared himself ready to guide a party to the beach opposite the place where the sloop lay.

Dinner was ready and waiting on board the *Transit*, but nobody thought of stopping to eat a mouthful after learning the news of what was taking place. The sole anxiety was to reach the beach as quickly as possible. The instant the stranger said he was ready, all hands, except those ordered to remain by the schooner, began to tumble into the available canoes, eager to be set ashore.

Poor Worth was sadly distressed when he heard of the terrible task undertaken by his friend, but he tried to cheer himself and the others by declaring that if any boat could live outside it was the canoe *Psyche*, and if any living sailor could carry her through the seas, whose angry roar filled the air, it was Sumner Rankin.

In the mean time the brave young fellow who was the object of all this anxiety had reached the mouth of the creek. There, in a sheltered spot, he paused for a few minutes to take breath and make his final preparations for a plunge into the roaring breakers outside.

He set taut the foot steering-gear, took double reefs in both his sails, saw that the halyards were clear and ready for instant service, adjusted the rubber apron so that the least possible water should enter the cockpit, and then, with a firm grasp of his paddle, he shoved off.

In another minute he was breasting the huge, combing breakers of the outer bar, and working with desperate energy to force his frail craft through or over them. The roar of waters was deafening, while the fierce gusts rendered breathing difficult. At one moment the sharp bow of the canoe would point vaguely towards the sky, while the next would see it directed into a watery abyss, and plunging downward as though never to rise again. At such moments the rudder would be lifted from the water, and only the most skilful use of the paddle prevented the canoe from broaching to and being rolled over and over, to be finally dashed in fragments on the beach. Again and again the wave crests broke on her deck, sweeping her fore and aft with a blinding mass of hissing water.

Still the boy's strength held out, still his paddle was wielded with regular strokes, and finally he came off victorious in this first bout of his fierce, single-handed struggle. The line of breakers was passed, and riding over the comparatively regular seas beyond, he began working dead to windward for an offing.

Not until he was a good half-mile off shore, and very nearly exhausted by his tremendous efforts, did he push back the rubber apron, drop his centre-board, and then, steadying the canoe with his paddle, seize a favorable opportunity for hoisting the tiny after-sail that should keep her momentarily headed into the wind. Then, quickly unjointing his paddle and thrusting its parts into the cockpit, he grasped the halyard, and with a single pull set the double-reefed main-sail.

Now was a most critical moment, for as he pulled in on the main-sheet, and the sail began to feel the full force of the wind, the little craft heeled over gunwale under. Only by promptly scrambling to the weather-deck, and sitting with his feet braced under the lee coaming, while his whole body was thrown out far over the side, did he prevent her from capsizing. Then she gathered headway and dashed forward. With one hand on the deck tiller, and holding the main-sheet in the other, the boy peered anxiously ahead.

Yes, there was the wreck! Oh, so far away! with clouds of white spray dashing high above it. Could he ever reach it through those tumultuous seas? Lifting him high in the air, where he was exposed to the full force of the wind at one moment, they towered above the deep trough into which he sank at the next, and left his bits of sails shaking as if in a calm. With full confidence in himself and his boat, he believed he could reach it—and he did.

He had no time to look at the anxious watchers on the beach, but they noted his every movement with painful eagerness. They almost held their breath as some huge wave tossed him high aloft, and again as he was completely hidden from them behind its foam-capped crest. At length they saw him reach a point abreast the wreck, round sharply to under its lee, and seize his paddle. In another minute he was on board, with the first half of his task accomplished.

He found Rust Norris crouching in the lee of the little deck-house, nearly exhausted with pain, hours of cold drenching, and the terror of his position. The wreck was trembling so violently with each shock of the seas that it seemed as though she must break up beneath their feet.

Rust's left arm was supported in a rude sling made from a strip of his shirt knotted about his neck. He did not speak as the boy bent over him, but an expression of glad surprise and renewed hope lighted his haggard face.

"Come, Rust," shouted Sumner; "with one big effort you'll be all right. They are waiting

"HE FOUND RUST NORRIS CROUCHING IN THE LEE OF THE LITTLE DECK-HOUSE."

for you on the beach, and the canoe will carry you that far easy enough, if you can only manage to get into her. You will have to sit low down and steer with your feet while you hold the sheet in your hand. All you'll have to do is to run her in dead before the wind, head on for the beach."

With infinite difficulty the wounded man was finally seated in the narrow cockpit of the frail craft. A moment later it was shoved off from the trembling wreck, and was racing with fearful speed towards the beach. It seemed to leap from the top of one huge wave to the next without sinking into the intervening hollow. Not until it was dragged safely ashore by those who rushed into the breakers to meet the flying craft did Rust Norris realize that he was her sole occupant.

Chapter XXI.

SUMNER'S SELF-SACRIFICE.

If Rust Norris had not been rendered so nearly helpless by his broken arm, Sumner would have endeavored to make the *Psyche* bear them both safely to land, if not by carrying them, at least by supporting them while they swam alongside. On his way to the wrecked sloop he had thought that perhaps this might be done, but as soon as he discovered Rust's real condition he knew that he might as well leave him there to drown as to attempt to burden the light craft with their double weight. At that moment the lad made up his mind that Rust should have the canoe to himself, and that he would take whatever chance of escape still remained. Thus he had resolutely shoved the canoe off, with its single occupant, while he stayed behind, clinging to the leeward mast-stay, and watching with eager eyes the perilous passage to the beach of the man for whom he had risked so much. The act was a bit of that coolly-planned self-sacrificing heroism that stamps true bravery, and distinguishes it from recklessness.

A Story of the Everglades.

In his exhausted and partially dazed condition, Rust did not realize the sacrifice made by his young deliverer until the canoe had been snatched from the breakers by a dozen willing hands, and drawn high on the beach beyond their cruel grasp. Then, on looking for the boy and seeing that he had remained behind, he uttered a great cry, and sank down limp and helpless on the wet sand.

Those on shore had seen from the first that only one was coming in the canoe, while one was left behind, but they had not known which was approaching them until the *Psyche* was dragged from the breakers.

Worth was in an agony of despair at his friend's peril. "Let me go to him!" he cried. "I would rather drown than stand here without trying to save him!"

"No; let me go! Let me go!" cried the others; and they made frantic attempts to again launch the canoe through the breakers; but they might as well have tried to launch it through a stone wall. Again and again was it hurled back, while those who strove to launch it were torn from their footing and flung upon the beach.

Then there was a shout of "Here he comes! He is in the water!" and then they strained their eyes in vain for another glimpse of their well-loved young comrade.

Sumner had indeed taken the plunge, but not voluntarily. He had determined to remain by the sloop until she broke up and he was compelled to swim, or until the falling tide should render the passage of that seething maelstrom less terrible. Thus thinking, he was about to seek the poor shelter in which he had found Rust, when a great wave, rushing over the wreck, swept him from it, and buried him beneath tons of its mighty volume.

As he came gasping to the surface he was again almost immediately overwhelmed and borne under. Still, he had drawn a breath of air, and had noted the direction of the beach. He knew that, sooner or later, alive or dead, the waves would cast him ashore. So, without trying to swim forward, he devoted all his energies to reaching the surface, and breathing as often as possible. It seemed as though he were merely rising and sinking, without moving forward an inch, and it required all his self-control to keep from exhausting himself by violent struggles to make a perceptible headway. He retained his presence of mind, however, and after a half-hour of battle the very waves seemed to acknowledge his victory, and tossed him up within sight of the watchers, who had given up all hope except that of finding his lifeless body.

They uttered a glad shout; but it was checked as he was again buried from their sight. Again he appeared, and this time much nearer. Then Lieutenant Carey rushed into the water. Behind him Worth, Quorum, and the others formed a line, tightly grasping each other's hands, and at length the swimmer was within their reach.

With cries of exultant joy, they bore him up the beach and laid him on the sand; but their rejoicing was quickly succeeded by consternation. He lay with closed eyes, cold, and apparently lifeless.

"Hurry to the schooner, Worth, and tell them to have hot water, hot blankets, and a roaring fire ready by the time we get there," demanded the Lieutenant. "We will bring him as quickly as possible."

For hours they worked over the senseless form of the brave lad. So nearly had the sea accomplished its cruel purpose that, but for the lessons learned by the workers years before at Annapolis, Sumner Rankin's life would have been given in exchange for that of Rust Norris. At length a faint color tinged his cheeks, a faint breath came from between his lips, and they knew that their efforts had not been in vain. An hour later he was sleeping quietly, and it was certain that Nature would complete the work of restoration. Then the same skill that had snatched life from apparent death was directed to the setting and proper bandaging of Rust's broken arm.

The Norther continued to blow all that night and the following day, and during this period of enforced idleness Sumner was not allowed to leave his berth. His every want was anticipated, and those who surrounded him vied with each other in their tender care of the lad who had so well won their regard and admiration. As for Rust Norris, his whole nature seemed to have undergone such a change that his former intimates would hardly have recognized him. He sat and watched constantly beside the boy to whom he owed so much, and could hardly be persuaded to leave him for the briefest intervals.

During that second day of storm he made a full confession of how and why he had attempted to thwart the objects of Lieutenant Carey's expedition. His enmity had been particularly directed towards Sumner, and when the latter instead of himself had been chosen to pilot the *Transit* up the reef, he had formed a plan of revenge that he immediately proceeded to carry out. This was to visit the Everglade Indians, and inform them that the expedition was for the purpose of spying out their lands and preparing for their removal to a far-away country of cold and snow, where they would certainly die. To accomplish this he had joined a Bahama smuggler, and with a cask of rum as a cargo, they had sailed in the small sloop owned by the latter for Cape Sable. Here they met a party of Indians who had come down from the 'Glades on a deer-hunt, and after plying them with rum, roused them to anger by their lying tale concerning the coming expedition. The Indians had departed to spread the report to the rest of their band, and to devise plans for frustrating the supposed purpose of the expedition. Their departure had taken place on the day of the *Transit's* arrival on the coast, and but for the signs of the appoaching Norther, Rust Norris and his companion would have left the lagoon in which they were so snugly anchored that afternoon. Noting these signs they decided to remain where they were until it should blow over. They had no idea when the *Transit* would reach the cape, nor did they suppose that Sumner was aware of the passage into the lagoon. It was therefore with surprise and consternation that they found those whom they had attempted to injure anchored close beside them. They at once determined to take advantage of the darkness to run out of the lagoon before the storm broke, and seek another shelter among the mangrove keys a short distance farther inland.

They slipped their cable, not daring to lift the anchor for fear the sound might be heard on board the schooner, and drifted down to the mouth of the creek with the last of the ebb-tide. Here, while waiting for a breeze, Rust conceived the idea of effectually crippling the expedition by stealing their boats, and went back up the creek for that purpose. He cut them loose from the schooner and attempted to tow them silently down to where the sloop lay, but as the tide had turned and was flooding strongly up the creek, he found it impossible to do so. So he turned them adrift in the belief that they would be driven to the farther side of the lagoon, and dashed to pieces by the storm that was about to break. At any rate, the expedition would be so long delayed in recovering their boats that the news of their coming would be spread over the length and breadth of the Everglades before they could enter them.

So much time had thus been wasted that before the sloop could be taken to the proposed place of safety the storm burst in all its fury. They were forced to seek refuge in another place that was partially exposed, but where with two anchors they could probably have ridden out the gale. With but one, they were dragged from their moorings soon after daylight, and driven on the reef where the sloop now lay. Rust's arm had been broken by the gybing of the main boom, and, left alone, exposed to the fury of those raging seas, he had given up all hope long before Sumner came to his rescue.

"And to think," said Rust, in conclusion, "that the fellow to whom I was doing all this meanness should have come after me and offered to throw away his own life to save mine! I tell you, gentlemen, it makes me feel meaner 'n a toad-fish!"

Chapter XXII.

GOOD-BYE TO THE *TRANSIT*

That night the Norther broke, and by the following morning the weather was of that absolutely perfect character that makes the winter the most delightful season of the year in southern Florida. The sun shone with unclouded splendor, fish leaped from the clear waters, gay-plumaged birds flitted among the mangroves, and made the air vocal with their happy songs. All nature was full of life and rejoicing.

Although Lieutenant Carey was much disturbed by learning that false reports had been spread among the Indians concerning the nature of his expedition, and realized that its difficulties would be greatly increased thereby, he had no thought of abandoning it. Therefore, by the earliest daylight, preparations were made for repairing the damaged cruisers, and putting them in condition for a new start. The stanch little *Psyche* had been brought down the beach the day before. There was a good supply of tools aboard the schooner, and Sumner, who had fully recov-

REPAIRING THE "PUNKIN' SEED"

ered his strength, was found to be so expert a shipwright that he was intrusted with planning and directing the repairs to the cruisers, while the Lieutenant, with several men, went to examine into the condition of the wrecked sloop, and see what could be done with her.

They found her injuries so much less than was expected, that within three days she had been hauled off the reef and rendered sufficiently seaworthy for the voyage back to Key West.

In this time also Sumner finished his job on the cruisers, and they were again in thorough order for the work required of them.

Rust Norris was able to render them one service, by guiding them to some cisterns from which they obtained the supply of fresh-water, without which they would not have dared proceed on their cruise. His companion, who was a good hunter and well acquainted with the game resorts of that vicinity, provided them with plenty of fresh venison. He also won Worth's regard by giving him a turkey call, or whistle, made from one of the wing-bones of a wild turkey, and taking him off before daylight one morning on a turkey hunt. From this the boy returned fully as proud as the fine gobbler he had shot had been a short time before. So elated was he by this success that he declared himself to be the hunter of the expedition from that time forth, and promised to provide it with all necessary meat.

By the close of the third day after the storm everything was in readiness for a new start. That evening was spent in writing letters to be sent back by the sloop, and daylight of the following morning saw both vessels standing out of the lagoon. Once outside, the sloop bore away to the westward, its occupants waving their hats and shouting good wishes to those whom but a few days before they had tried their best to injure.

"I declare!" said Sumner to Worth, "I don't know of anything that makes a fellow feel better than to succeed in turning an enemy into a friend. Now I shall always like Rust Norris, and he will always like me, while if no difficulty had arisen between us we might have been on speaking terms all our lives without caring particularly for each other."

"But, Sumner!" exclaimed Worth, in a grieved tone, "aren't you ever going to care particularly for me, because we have never been enemies?"

"Care for you, old man! After all we have gone through with together, and after all the anxiety we have had on account of each other? Why, Worth, if I cared any more for you than I do, I'd pack you up in cotton and send you home by express, for fear you might get hurt."

"Then please don't," laughed the boy, "for I want to see the Everglades, and do some more hunting before I am sent home."

Although Worth was so impatient to see the 'Glades, and though the *Transit* was headed directly for them, he was obliged to content himself with seeing other things for some days to come. For a whole week the little schooner threaded her way through the most bewildering maze of islands, reefs, and channels known to this continent. There were thousands of keys of all sizes and shapes, and all covered with the mangroves that had built them. As for the oyster bars, sand-bars, and reefs, they were so numerous that, in finding her way through them, the *Transit* was headed to every point, half-point, and quarter-point of the compass during each hour of her sailing time. The number of times that she ran aground were innumerable, as were those that she was compelled to turn back from some blind channel and seek a new one.

Through all this bewildering maze of keys and channels great tide rivers of crystal water continually ebbed and flowed. In them uncounted millions of fish, from huge silvery tarpon, vampirelike devil-fish, and ravenous sharks, down to tiny fellows, striped, spotted, or mottled with every hue of the rainbow, rushed and sported, chased and being chased, devouring and being devoured, but always affording a fascinating kaleidoscope of darting forms and flashing colors.

Nor was the bird-life of these Ten Thousand Islands less interesting. It seemed as though the numbers of the great Wader and Soarer families collected here were almost as many as the fish on which they feasted. Whole regiments of stately flamingoes, clad in their pink hunting-coats, stood solemnly on the mud-flats. Squadrons of snow-white pelicans sailed in company with fleets of their more soberly plumaged comrades. Great snowy herons, little white herons, great blue herons, little blue herons, green herons, and yellow-legged herons mingled with cranes and curlews on the oyster-bars. Ducks of infinite variety, together with multitudes of coots and cormorants, floated serenely on the placid waters. Overhead, clouds of snowy ibises, outlined in pink by edgings of roseate spoon-bills, rose and fell and glinted in the bright sunlight. Gannets, gulls, and ospreys hovered above the fishing-grounds. Bald-headed eagles watched them from the tops of tall mangroves, ready at a moment's notice to pounce down and rob them of their prey. Far overhead, black specks against the brilliant blue of the sky, sailed, on motionless pinions, stately men-of-war hawks or frigate-birds—most graceful of all the soarers. All these, and many more, the mere naming of which would fill a chapter, flocked to these teeming fishing-grounds, and afforded a never-ending source of wonder and amusement to our young canoe-mates and their companions.

Still, with all these, besides the unending difficulties of the navigation to occupy their minds, the end of a week found the boys heartily tired of mangrove keys and blind channels, and anxious for a change of scene. It was, therefore, with a feeling of decided relief that a dark, unbroken line, stretching north and south as far as the eye could reach, was finally sighted and pronounced to be the pine woods of the main-land. Approaching it with infinite difficulty on account of the rapidly shoaling water, they at length discovered a large stream, the water of which was brackish. It was evidently one of the numerous waterways draining the vast reservoirs of the 'Glades into the sea. Here the exploring party was to leave the *Transit* and take to the smaller craft, in which they proposed to penetrate the interior.

Again an evening was devoted to writing letters to be sent back by the schooner, and again all hands were ordered to turn out by daylight.

Lieutenant Carey had decided to send one of the cruisers back, and to take but one besides the three canoes into the 'Glades. The recent difficulties of navigation had shown him that a full crew would be needed to carry the schooner back to deep water, and he also imagined that the fewer boats the explorers had to force through the 'Glades the easier they would get along. The Indians, too, would be less suspicious of a small party than of a large one. Thus he decided to limit the party to himself and the two boys in the canoes, with Quorum and one other man in the cruiser, or five in all.

With a breakfast by lamplight, and the final preparations hurried as much as possible, the sun was just rising when the little fleet shoved off from the *Transit*, and with flashing paddles entered the mouth of the dark-looking river, the waters of which, in all probability, the keels of white men's boats were now to furrow for the first time.

"Good-bye, Mr. Sloe! You want to hurry round to Cape Florida, or we'll be there first!"

"Good-bye, Quorum! Look out for that woolly scalp of yours!" came from the schooner.

"Good-bye! Good-luck! Good-bye!" and then the canoes rounded a wooded point, and were lost to sight of those who watched their first plunge into the trackless wilderness.

Chapter XXIII.

WORTH MEETS A PANTHER.

To find themselves once more in their canoes, and to be gliding over unknown waters, with new scenes unfolding at every turn, was so exhilarating to the boys that they started up the river at racing speed, shouting and laughing as they went. They were about to disappear from the sight of the others around a bend of the stream when they were checked by a shout from Lieutenant Carey. As he joined them he said:

"We must keep together, boys, and regulate our speed by that of the cruiser, for, in case of unforeseen difficulties or dangers, it won't do for us to be separated. I wouldn't make any more noise than is necessary either. There is no knowing what the Indians, whose country we are entering, may take it into their heads to do. While I do not anticipate any serious trouble from them, I would rather avoid them as much as possible, and by proceeding quietly we may escape their notice—at least for the present."

For the first mile or two the river-banks were hidden beneath a dense growth of mangroves, though above these they could catch occasional glimpses of the tops of pines and tall palmettoes. The mangroves grew smaller and thinner, until finally they disappeared entirely, and on tasting the water over which they floated our voyagers found it to be fresh and sweet.

"There is no danger of our suffering from thirst on this trip whatever may happen," said Sumner.

They were close to one of the banks as he spoke, and from it there suddenly came a rushing sound, followed by the floundering splash of some huge body in the water, so close at hand that their canoes were violently rocked by the waves that immediately followed. The suddenness of the whole proceeding drew a startled cry from Worth.

"What could it have been?" he asked in a low tone, and with a very white face. "Was it a hippopotamus, do you think?" He had seen the "hippos" splash into their tank in Central Park.

"Not exactly," laughed Sumner, who, after a slight start, had quickly regained his composure. "It was a big alligator, and he went so close under my canoe that I could have touched him with the paddle."

"Suppose he had upset us?"

"There wasn't any danger of that; he was more scared than we were, but he knew enough to dive clear of us."

"But if he should take it into his head to attack us?"

"He won't, though. Mr. Alligator is a great coward. If he is disturbed while taking a sun-bath on shore, he makes a blind rush for the water in spite of all obstacles, but it is only because he is too frightened to do anything else. Once safely in the water, he is glad enough to sink quietly to the bottom without seeking the further acquaintance of his enemies. That has always been my experience with them, but then I have only known them where they were hunted a good deal. The fellows where we are going may be bolder, but I have never heard of alligators being anything but awful cowards."

Partly reassured by this, Worth regarded the next alligator that he saw with greater composure, and before the day was over he hardly minded them at all. He certainly had an opportunity of becoming familiar with them, for they fairly swarmed in the river. Nearly every sand-spit showed from one to a dozen of them, of all sizes, lying motionless in the warm sunlight.

Worth declared that some of them were twenty feet long; but Sumner laughed at him, and said that twelve or thirteen feet at most would be nearer the mark. In this statement he was supported by Lieutenant Carey, who said that even a fifteen-foot alligator would be a monster, and he doubted if one of that length had ever been seen.

Most of the scaly brutes, after finding themselves safely in the water, would rise to the surface for one more look at the cause of their fright. In thus rising, they only displayed the tops of their heads, and as the canoes approached these would imperceptibly sink until only four black spots, indicating the eyes and nostrils, were visible. Then these, too, would disappear without leaving the faintest ripple to mark the place where they had been. Often a quick spurt would take the canoes to the spot in time for the boys to look down through the clear water and see the great black body lying motionless on the bottom, or darting swiftly away towards some safer hiding-place.

Sometimes they saw tiny fellows, brightly marked with yellow, and but recently hatched, sunning themselves on broad lily-pads. These were never found in company with their elders, which, Lieutenant Carey said, was because their papas were too fond of eating them.

A Story of the Everglades.

When Sumner spoke of alligators' eggs and nests, Worth asked, innocently, if the mother alligators sat on their eggs like hens.

At the mental picture thus presented Sumner laughed so heartily that he could hardly wield his paddle, but Lieutenant Carey explained that an alligator's nest is built of sticks, leaves, and grass, very like a musk-rat's house. "In the middle of this," he said, "are laid from twenty to forty thick-shelled, pure white eggs, about the size of the largest goose-eggs. These are left to be hatched by the heat of the sun and of the decomposing mass surrounding them. When they break their shells, the little fellows immediately scramble for the nearest water, where they are left to care for themselves without a suggestion of parental guidance or advice. In fact, they are wise enough from the very first to keep out of the way of their elders, whose only love for them seems to be that of an epicure for a dainty dish."

"Aren't there crocodiles, too, in Florida?" asked Sumner.

"Yes. Professor Hornaday mentions genuine crocodiles as being found in Biscayne Bay, on the east coast, where I hope we shall get a look at them. They are described as differing from alligators in the head, that of the crocodile being narrower and longer. The snout is sharper than that of an alligator, and at the end of the lower jaw are two long canine teeth or tusks that project through holes in the upper lip."

"Him big fighter, too," remarked Quorum from the cruiser. "Him heap mo' wicked dan de 'gator. De Injun call him 'Allapatta hajo,' an' say hit mean mad 'gator."

As the party advanced up the stream the current became so much stronger that the boys began to feel the effects of their steady paddling against it, and were no longer inclined to shoot ahead of the others. The foliage of the banks changed with each mile, and by noon the pines had given place to clumps of palmetto, bay, water-oak, wild fig, mastic, and other timber. Here and there were grassy glades, in more than one of which they caught tantalizing glimpses of vanishing white-tailed deer.

The water began to assume an amber tint, and was so brilliantly clear that in looking down through it they could see great masses of coral rocks that often overshadowed the yawning mouths of dark chasms. Above these, whole meadows of the most beautiful grasses—red, green, purple, and yellow—streamed and waved with the ceaseless motion of the current. Schools of bright-hued fish darted through and over these, and turtles, plumping into the water from stranded logs or sunny sand-spits, could be seen scuttling away to their hiding-places among them.

The noontide heat of the sun was intense as the signal for a halt was given. The boats were turned in towards a bank where a grass-plot, shaded by a clump of rustling palmettoes, offered a tempting resting-place.

As they landed, Worth was certain that he saw a flock of turkeys disappear in a small hammock back of the clearing. With his new-born hunting instinct strong within him, he seized his gun and crossed the glade, in the hope of getting a shot. He had practised constantly on the call given him by his instructor, and now felt competent to deceive even the most experienced gobbler. Advancing cautiously within cover of the hammock, and seating himself on a log that was completely concealed by a screen of bushes, he began to call, "Keouk, keouk, keouk." For ten minutes or so he repeated the sounds at short intervals without getting a reply. Suddenly, a slight rustle in the bushes behind him caused Worth to turn his head. Within a yard of him glared a pair of cruel green eyes.

With a yell of terror the boy dropped his gun, sprang to his feet, burst from the bushes, and fled wildly towards camp. Reaching it in safety, but hatless and breathless, he declared that a tiger had been crouched, and just about to spring at him.

"Perhaps it was a 'coon," suggested Sumner.

"'Coon, indeed?" cried Worth, hotly. "If you had seen the size of its eyes, you would have thought it was an elephant!"

"What has become of your gun?" inquired the Lieutenant.

"I haven't the slightest idea," replied the boy; "and I don't care. I wouldn't face those eyes again for a thousand guns."

Finally, however, he was persuaded to return with Lieutenant Carey and Sumner, both well armed, and point out the scene of his fright. They found his hat, the gun, and the log on which he had been sitting. Then in the soft earth close behind it they also found a double set of huge panther tracks—one made while cautiously approaching the supposed turkey, and the other while bounding away in affright at Worth's yell.

"I don't wonder that you were both frightened," said the Lieutenant, with a smile; "but now that your skill as a turkey-caller is established, I wouldn't go out on a hunting expedition alone again if I were you."

"Indeed I won't, sir. I'd rather never see another turkey than risk being stared at by such a pair of eyes as that panther carries round with him."

Chapter XXIV.

RATTLESNAKES AND RIFLE-SHOTS.

While they were returning through the grassy glade, the Lieutenant, who was a few steps in advance, suddenly stopped and sprang back. The boys barely caught a glimpse of a flat, wicked-looking head, from which a forked tongue was viciously thrusting, and heard a sound like the whir-r-r-r of an immense locust, when Lieutenant Carey fired, and the head disappeared in the tall grass.

"It was a snake, wasn't it?" asked Worth.

"Worse than that," replied the Lieutenant. "It was a diamond-back rattler, the most venomous snake known to this country, and with another step I should have been on him. I'd rather face your panther unarmed than to have stepped on that fellow."

"What would you have done if you had met it without a gun in your hand?" asked Sumner, curiously.

"Run," answered the Lieutenant, laconically, as he grasped the lifeless body of the snake by the tail, with a view to dragging it into camp.

"But if he had caught and bitten you?"

"He wouldn't have caught me, because, in the first place, he would have been content to be let alone, and wouldn't have chased me. In the second place, the rattlesnake is such a sluggish reptile that I could run faster than he, and could easily have kept out of his way."

"Well, then, what would you do if you were bitten?"

"If it were on an arm or a leg, I should tie my handkerchief above the wound, and twist it with a bit of stick as tightly as possible, so as to impede the circulation. Then I should enlarge the wound with my knife, and, if I could reach it with my mouth, I should suck it for five minutes, frequently spitting out the blood. After that I should get to camp as quickly as possible, put a freshly-chewed tobacco plaster on the wound every ten minutes for the next hour, and at the same time drink a tumblerful of whiskey or other alcoholic liquor. If I could do all that, and the fangs had not struck an artery, I should feel reasonably sure of recovery."

"Suppose they had struck an artery, what would you do?"

"Reconcile myself to death as quickly as possible, for I should probably be dead inside of three minutes," was the grim reply.

Worth shuddered as he gazed at the scaly body that, marked with black and yellow diamonds, trailed for more than five feet behind the Lieutenant, and remarked that the sooner they got away from the haunts of panthers and rattlesnakes, and back among the good-natured alligators, the better he should like it.

"I shouldn't think Indians would care to live in such a rattlesnaky country," he added.

"They don't mind them," laughed the Lieutenant. "Their keen eyesight generally enables them to discover a snake as soon as he sees them. Then, too, they have an infallible antidote for snake bite, the secret of which they refuse to divulge to white men."

"How many rattles has this fellow?" asked Sumner.

"Only seven," answered Lieutenant Carey, counting them.

"Then he was a young fellow. I thought from his size that he must be pretty old, and would have twelve or thirteen rattles and a button at least."

"The number of rattles does not indicate a snake's age," said the Lieutenant, smiling. "They get broken off, as do long finger-nails.

I have seen very large snakes with fewer rattles than others that were smaller and evidently younger."

While they were eating lunch Quorum skinned the snake, rubbed the beautiful skin thoroughly with fine salt, and rolled it into a compact bundle, in which condition it would keep for a long time.

After lunch and the hour's rest that followed it the little fleet was again got under way, and proceeded up the swift river. About the middle of the afternoon they entered the broad belt of cypress timber that borders the Everglades on the west. Here the serried ranks of tall trees, stretching away as far as the eye could reach, held out their long moss-draped arms until they met overhead, and formed a dim archway for the passage of the rushing current. The water flowed with strange gurglings against the gray trunks, and the whole scene was one of such weird solitude, that on entering it the explorers shivered as with a chill. Through the semi-twilight fluffy night herons flitted like gray shadows, and the harsh scream of an occasional water-fowl, startled by the dip of paddles, echoed through the gloomy forest like a cry of human distress.

The atmosphere of the place was so depressing

that no one spoke, but each bent to his paddle or oars with redoubled energy, the quicker to escape into the sunshine that they knew must lie somewhere beyond it.

Quorum, who had been sitting in the stern of the cruiser while the sailor rowed, was finally made so nervous by his uncanny surroundings that he begged his companion to change places with him. He wished to row that his thoughts might be occupied with the hard work. The sailor complied, though laughing at the negro's fears as he did so. While Quorum was working with desperate energy to catch up with the other boats, there came an incident of so startling a nature that in relating it afterwards he said: "I tell yo, sah, de ole niggah so skeer dat him come de neares' in he life to tu'nin' plumb white!"

It was a volley of rifle-shots that flashed and roared from the forest on the right bank of the river like thunder from a clear sky. A second volley followed almost immediately, and then succeeded such a din of yells, whoops, and howlings as would have dismayed the stoutest heart.

For an instant each one of the explorers imagined himself to be the sole survivor of a wholesale massacre, and the surprise of the volleys was fully equalled by that of seeing his companions still alive.

"A VOLLEY OF RIFLE-SHOTS FLASHED AND ROARED FROM THE FOREST."

While the echoes of the first volley were still reverberating through the dim arches of the forest, Quorum whirled the cruiser around as on a pivot, and despite his companion's remonstrances, started her down the river with a rush. The canoemen sat for a couple of seconds with uplifted paddles as though paralyzed, and in that space of time the powerful current did for them what Quorum had done for the cruiser. There seemed nothing to do but to fly from those crashing rifles and demoniac yells. So fly they did, paddling furiously, and casting fearful glances over their shoulders to note if they were pursued. It must be stated, however, that the Lieutenant tried repeatedly to rally the fugitives, and when he found this to be impossible, he held his own canoe in check until certain that no immediate pursuit was being undertaken.

It was nearly sunset when he overtook the others at a place beyond the lower edge of the cypress belt, where they had halted to wait for him. He found them still badly demoralized, and ready to continue their flight at the first intimation of further danger.

"Well, boys," he cried, cheerily, as his canoe swept down beside them, "I suppose we might as well call this the end of our day's work, and go into camp."

"Camp?" almost gasped Worth. "You don't mean, sir, that you propose to go into camp while the whole country is simply swarming with savage Indians?"

"I certainly do," replied the Lieutenant. "We shall be safer in camp, where we can work together, than on the river, where we must necessarily be separated, especially in the dark. Moreover, I don't believe we shall be molested here. The mere fact that they have not pursued us so far is, to my mind, an indication that they don't intend to. Indeed, boys, in thinking over this matter, I am inclined to believe that the Indians, or whoever fired those shots, for I didn't see a human being, only intended to frighten us, in the hope that we would give up our undertaking. I believe that the cartridges they fired were blanks. Certainly some of us would have been hit if they had been loaded. I cannot remember seeing a bullet strike the water or anywhere else; can you?"

No; none of them had noticed anything of the kind.

"That they have not pursued us is another indication that they do not desire our lives," continued the Lieutenant. "Besides all this, the Seminoles are fully aware of the consequences to themselves in case they should kill a white man, and I have no idea that they desire a war or anything like it. Thus I say that they only meant to frighten us, and I must acknowledge that they succeeded. I, for one, was never more startled and scared in my life. Now I propose that we camp here, without lighting a fire to betray our presence, or let them know that we have stopped running, until towards morning. Then I intend to try the passage of that cypress swamp again."

Chapter XXV.

WORTH'S LONELY NIGHT-WATCH.

Lieutenant Carey's remarks were received by his companions with considerable incredulity. None of them had ever been under fire before, and it was hard to realize that the deafening volleys that had roared at them from the cypress forest had not been fired with deadly intent. To be sure, neither they, nor even their boats, had been hit; but that might as easily be attributed to poor marksmanship as to good intention on the part of the Indians. Of course, they did not doubt for an instant that those who had fired from that well-concealed ambush were Indians. Who else occupied that country, or who else would have done such a thing? Had not Rust Norris given the Indians false information concerning the objects of the expedition, and roused them to anger against it? Even if this first attack had only been intended for a scare, would a second prove equally harmless? What possible chance had their little band of making its way through the trackless leagues between there and the eastern coast, if the four hundred or so of Seminoles occupying the country had determined to prevent them? None at all, of course.

On the other hand, as Lieutenant Carey very justly urged, the Indians could not afford to go to war with the whites. Besides, did the way ahead of them present any greater difficulties than that they had so recently traversed? What could they do with their frail boats, even if they should return to the open waters of the Gulf? Could they hope to reach Key West in them? Then, too, how humiliating it would be to give up their undertaking merely because they had been frightened, and without having caught a glimpse of their enemies!

Lieutenant Carey declared his purpose of going on alone if the others refused to accompany him, and Sumner said that, as the son of a naval officer, he was bound to follow the Lieutenant. Worth said: "Of course, if you go, Sumner, I must go with you; but I'm awfully frightened all the same."

The sailor said that he had no thought of disobeying the Lieutenant's orders, and only deserted him as he did in the cypress swamp because Quorum was at the oars, and carried him off against his will.

Quorum said: "Ef Marse Summer an' Marse Worf gwine fight dem Injuns, ob co'se de ole man gwine erlong to pertec' 'em. Dem chillun can't be 'lowed ter go prospeckin' in de wilderness wifout Quor'm ter look affer 'em, an' holp do de fightin' as well as de cookin'."

All this discussion took place after the canoes had been hauled from the water and concealed in a clump of bushes, and while coffee was being prepared over the alcohol lamps, which gave out great heat with little light. They gathered closely about their little stoves and talked in low tones, while the night shadows settled down and shut out the surrounding landscape. After eating a hearty meal, which showed their appetites to be in nowise impaired by their recent fright, and providing a supply of coffee for the morning, they rolled up in their blankets and lay down for a few hours' sleep on the bare ground. That is, all but Worth lay down. He, wrapping his blanket about him, and sitting with his gun across his knees, prepared to keep the first hour's watch. He was given this first hour because he was the youngest, and he was to wake Sumner when it had expired. Sumner was to rouse Quorum, he the sailor, and he the Lieutenant, who was to stand the last watch and decide upon the time for starting.

A Story of the Everglades. 195

To be sitting there alone, surrounded by the unseen terrors of a Southern wilderness, was a novel and weird experience for Worth. He could hear the eddying and gurgling of the river, with frequent splashes that marked the nocturnal activity of its animal life. Innumerable insects filled the air about him with shrill sounds, and deep-voiced frogs kept up a ceaseless din from the adjacent swamps. Frequent vibratory bellowings, exactly like those of an enraged bull, and certain flounderings in the water, attested the wakefulness of his newly-made alligator acquaintances. The forest rang with the tiresomely irritating notes of the chuck-wills-widows and the solemn warnings of the great hoot owls.

Every now and then he was startled by the agonized cries of some unfortunate bird seized and dragged from its resting-place by a 'coon or other predatory animal. These, loud and shrill at first, gradually became weaker, until hushed into a lifeless silence. His blood chilled at the distant howl of wolves, or the human-like cry of a panther, and it required all the boy's strength of mind to refrain from arousing his comrades long before the expiration of that interminable hour.

Only a frequent reaching out of the hand and touching Sumner, who lay close beside him, gave him courage to maintain his solitary vigil. His mind was so actively occupied by what he heard, and by listening for what he dreaded still more to hear—the dip of paddles or other sounds indicating the approach of human enemies, that he had not the slightest inclination to sleep. He never was more wide awake in his life, with all his senses more keenly alert, than during that hour. He wondered if, with all those uncanny sounds ringing in his ears, he should dare even to close his eyes when his turn for sleeping came. He kept track of the time by occasionally striking a match, and looking at his watch beneath the sheltering folds of his blanket.

When the time came to waken Sumner, he hated to do so; but realizing that his own strength for the ensuing day depended upon his sleeping that night, he finally laid his hand gently on his comrade's forehead. From long training in being aroused at unseemly hours, Sumner sat up, wide awake, in an instant. The boys exchanged a few whispered words, and then Worth lay down. He closed his eyes, determined to try and sleep, though without the least idea of being able to do so.

When he next opened them Lieutenant Carey was bending over him, and saying that it was three o'clock in the morning. It seemed impossible that he could have been asleep for hours, and as the boy sat up rubbing his eyes, he was certain that the Lieutenant must have made some mistake.

In spite of the darkness, which was still as intense as ever, the boats had been almost noiselessly got into the water, and Quorum had heated the coffee made the night before. A cup of this, hot and strong, roused the boy into a full wakefulness, and fifteen minutes later he was seated in his canoe, prepared once more to undertake the passage of the dreaded cypress belt. The Lieutenant led the way, Sumner and Worth, keeping as close together as possible, followed, and the cruiser, with muffled oars, brought up the rear.

If the cypress forest into which they almost immediately plunged had seemed weird and gloomy by daylight, how infinitely more so was it in the pitchy darkness by which it was now enshrouded! Still, the black walls of tree-trunks rising on each side could be distinguished from the surface of the river, and thus the voyagers were enabled to keep in the channel. The air was motionless, and heavy with dampness and the rank odors of decaying vegetation. The rush of waters, the plash of their paddles, and the unaccountable night sounds of the drenched forest, rang out with startling distinctness. They proceeded with the utmost caution, and uttered no word; but it seemed as though their progress must be apparent to any ear within a mile of them.

For two hours they worked steadily and without a pause. They felt that they must have passed the scene of their previous evening's adventure. They were certain of this when at length the cypresses began to grow smaller; and their branches no longer meeting overhead, a faint light began to show itself in the lane of sky thus disclosed. Now they knew that they must be approaching the confines of the belt, and that the open 'Glades must be close at hand. They breathed more freely than they had for hours, and with each foot of progress their spirits became lightened.

The stream which they were following began to branch off in various directions, and the strength of its current was sensibly diminished. By the time the light was sufficient for them to discern clearly surrounding objects, the cypress belt was behind them, and the limitless expanse of the open 'Glades stretched away in their front. On the very edge of the cypress forest was a tiny hammock surmounting a slight elevation of solid ground. As the little fleet was passing this, its several crews were beginning to exchange a few words of conversation for the first time since leaving their camp.

Suddenly their voices were hushed by something almost as startling as the rifle-shots of the previous evening. This time it was the sound of a loud voice, evidently that of a white man, not more than a few rods from them, calling:

"Come, you fellows, wake up! Here it is daylight, and no fire started yet."

The startled canoemen looked at each other wonderingly, and Sumner was about to utter a shout that would betray their presence when a warning sign from Lieutenant Carey restrained him. Beckoning them to follow him quietly, the Lieutenant led the way past the hammock from which the voice had issued, and into a thick clump of tall sawgrass, by which they were effectually concealed. Bidding them remain there until his return, and on no account betray their presence by sound or movement, he left them, and cautiously guided his canoe back to the hammock. Stepping lightly from it as it touched the land, he made his way quietly through the trees and bushes composing the hammock until, without being seen or heard, he could command a view of an open space in its centre.

About the smouldering ashes of a camp-fire

ten rough-looking characters, whom he at once recognized as South Florida cowboys, were sitting up, yawning and rubbing their eyes into wakefulness, or lay still stretched on the ground enveloped in the blankets that formed their beds.

As there was but little danger of their discovering him, the Lieutenant waited where he was, to learn something of their character from their conversation, before either showing himself or retiring without disclosing his presence.

"ROUGH-LOOKING CHARACTERS, WHOM HE AT ONCE RECOGNIZED AS SOUTH FLORIDA COWBOYS."

Chapter XXVI.

THE FLORIDA EVERGLADES.

PRESENTLY a man who was rebuilding the fire straightened up, and addressing one of the others, said:

"We're going to get out o' here to-day, ain't we, Bill?"

"Yes, you bet we are," was the answer. "We hain't got nothing more to stay yere in the swamps for, onless you think they might make another try for it, which I don't they will."

"Not much they won't, after the way they skedaddled when we-uns began to yell. Hi! how they did cut down-stream! I'll bet they hain't stopped yit. They must ha' reckoned the hull Seminole nation was layin' fur 'em. Ho! ho! ho! ha! ha! ha! Hit was the slickest job I ever did see!"

"You don't reckin they'll hanker arter wisitin' the 'Glades agin in a hurry, then?" asked another voice.

"Hanker fur the 'Glades? Not muchy, they won't. Why, they won't tetch foot to the main-land of the State of Fluridy again, not if they can holp it. Leastways, not so long as they's a Injun left in hit. Hit's been a hard trip and a mean job for us fellers, but hit 'll pay. The report thet ar Leftenant 'll make when he gits home 'll do mo' to'd gittin' the Seminoles moved outen the kentry than ennything that's happened sence the Fluridy wah. Now mosey round lively, boys. Let's have a b'ilin' o' coffee, an' light outen hyar."

Lieutenant Carey had heard all that he cared to, and, without betraying his presence to the cowboys, he softly retraced his steps to where the canoe lay, and a minute later rejoined his party. Only telling them that the sooner they put a respectable distance between themselves and that place the better, he led the way into the main stream, that still flowed with considerable force through the grass beds, and turned in the direction of its source. Not until they had gone a good two miles did he pause, and then there were several reasons for calling a halt.

One reason was that they were far enough beyond the reach of the cowboys to defy discovery, and he wished to tell his companions what he had overheard. Another was that the sun was rising, and it was time for breakfast; and a third was that their watery highway having come to an end, it was necessary to decide upon their future course.

A small stove was carried in the cruiser, and as there was now nothing but water, with grass growing in it, about them, it was brought into service. The canoes gathered closely around the larger craft, and while Quorum prepared breakfast, the Lieutenant related his recent adventure. In conclusion he said: "So you see, boys, our Indians turned out to be white men, and the shooting was only intended to scare us, after all."

"But I don't understand how they knew we were coming, or what they wanted to frighten us for, anyway," said Sumner, wearing a very puzzled expression.

"Neither did I at first," replied Lieutenant Carey; "but I remember now that a gentleman in Key West said the Florida cattlemen would be greatly put out on learning of my proposed expedition. He said that they were using every means, foul and fair, to have the Indians removed from the State, and that they would be bitterly opposed to having the Everglades set apart as a permanent reservation. He advised me to look out for them, and I laughed at him. Now I realize that some one must have sent the news to them, and they got up this party to head us off in such a way that the blame would be placed upon the Indians. Yes, it is clear enough now; but it was a bit of a puzzle at first."

"Well," said Worth, "it is a great relief to know that they were not Indians, and that we are safely past them, with no danger of their following us."

"It certainly is," replied the Lieutenant. "Though it will be a greater one to me really to meet Indians, as we must sooner or later, and have them treat us decently, or rather leave us alone."

Here Quorum interrupted the conversation with the announcement of, "Breakfus, sah." The amount of cooking that he had managed to accomplish with that one-lidded stove was wonderful. Besides coffee, he had prepared a great smoking pot of oatmeal, and a dish of crisply fried bacon to be eaten with their hardtack; while these things were disappearing, he prepared and fried a panful of flapjacks that were as light and delicate as though cooked by a ten-thousand-dollar *chef* on the most modern of ranges. Out-of-door camp cookery deserves to rank as one of the exact sciences, and Quorum as one of its masters.

The old negro found perfect happiness in watching the relish with which his deftly prepared food was eaten, and his whole body expressed a smiling satisfaction at the words of praise lavished upon his skill. While Quorum was eating his own breakfast and the sailor was washing and stowing the dishes, the others stood up to take observations.

The main stream came to an end where they were, and from it a dozen narrow channels, filled with flags and lily-pads, or "bonnets," as they are called in Florida, radiated in as many directions. As far as the eye could reach, and infinitely farther, in front of them and on both sides, stretched a vast plain of coarse brown grass, rising to a height of several feet, and growing in a foot or two of limpid water. Innumerable channels of deeper water, marked by the vivid green of their peculiar vegetation, crossed and recrossed each other in every direction, and formed a bewildering net-work. The limitless brown level was dotted here and there with heavily timbered islands of all sizes, from a few rods to many acres in extent. Near at hand these were of a bright green, in the middle distance they were of a rich purple hue, and on the far horizon a misty blue. The highest of these islands, as well as the largest one visible, rose on the very limit of their vision, in the north-east, and as it formed a conspicuous landmark, they decided to lay a course for it. Accordingly, in single file, with the *Hu-la-lah* leading and "de *Punkin Seed*" bringing up the rear, the little fleet entered the narrow path that seemed to lead in that direction, and the journey was resumed.

The clearness of the water in the Everglades is accounted for by the fact that it flows above a bottom of coralline rock, and is always in motion. In it stagnation is unknown; and though it is everywhere crowded with plant life, it is as sweet and pure as that of a spring. Another curious fact about the Everglades which is generally unknown is that within their limits but few mosquitoes are found. During the summer months, when all residents on the coast of southern Florida, even the light-keepers away out on the reef, miles from land, are driven nearly crazy by these pests, the Seminoles, who retire to the Everglades to escape them, are rarely annoyed. The chief insect pests of the 'Glades are the midges, or stinging gnats, that swarm for an hour or so at sunset and sunrise. Against these the Indians protect themselves by smudges and by nettings of cheese-cloth.

From the difficulties of navigation experienced during this their first day in the 'Glades, our explorers realized that in striving to journey across their width they had undertaken a most arduous task. The channels that they attempted to follow seemed to lead in every direction but the right one. They were generally so narrow and choked with bonnets that paddling or rowing was impossible, and the boats must be forced ahead by poling. Every now and then, too, the shallow waters sank to an unknown depth that no pole could fathom. In such a case, if one attempted to pull his canoe along by grasping the tough grass stalks on either side of him, he was rewarded by a painful cut that often penetrated to the bone. It did not require many sad experiences of this kind to teach the boys that sawgrass is not to be handled with impunity. It has a triangular blade, provided with minutely serrated edges that, green or dry, cut like razors. While it ordinarily attains a height of but four or five feet, the great Everglade lake, Okeechobee, is surrounded by a barrier of "big sawgrass" that is wellnigh impenetrable to man or beast. Even the scaly-hided alligators shun it. This big sawgrass attains the thickness of a cornstalk, with a height of ten or twelve feet, is closely matted, and its cutting edges are possessed of the keenness of Oriental scimitars.

Sometimes the narrow channels along which our canoemates poled with such difficulty opened into broad clear spaces, where sailing was possible for a mile or so. Full as often the channels ended abruptly in the grass, when the only thing to do was to get overboard in water waist-deep, and push the boats through it.

The sun poured down with an intolerable glare, but its heat was tempered by the strong, fresh breeze that blows every day and all day over the 'Glades with the utmost regularity.

As they slowly drew near the island for which they were steering, it gradually assumed a conical shape and the symmetrical proportions of a pyramid. Late in the afternoon, while they were still about a mile from it, a dense volume of smoke suddenly arose from its extreme summit. This as suddenly disappeared, and then reappeared again at intervals of a second.

"I wonder if it can be a volcano?" queried Worth, as they gazed curiously at this phenomenon.

Chapter XXVII.

A PREHISTORIC EVERGLADE MOUND.

The whole party had come to a halt on first seeing the mysterious smoke, and now, with their boats grouped close together, they watched it curiously. Its several puffs did not last more than a minute, and then it was seen no more. Nobody but Worth mentioned volcanoes, and his suggestion caused a general smile. Quorum uttered the single word, "Injuns," and Lieutenant Carey agreed with him. He said:

"Such a smoke as that must result from human agency, and as I do not believe there is a white man besides ourselves within the limits of the 'Glades, it is probably the work of Indians, and is doubtless a signal of some kind, referring to our presence. I hope it is, for one of the objects of my mission being to reassure the Everglade Indians of the kindly intentions of the Government towards them, I shall be glad to meet them as quickly as possible. Let us go on, then, and have our first interview with them by daylight."

Half an hour later the canoes reached the island, close to which was a wide channel of open water that apparently extended wholly around it. So dense was its encircling growth of custard-apple and cocoa-plum bushes, that not until they had cut a passage through these could they reach the dry land behind them.

Anxious to discover the occupants of the island before darkness should set in, the Lieutenant, taking Sumner and the sailor with him, and leaving Worth and Quorum to guard the boats, set out for the mound, which, rising to a height of fifty or sixty feet, seemed to occupy the centre of the island.

Besides being desirous of meeting with Indians, Lieutenant Carey was most curious concerning the formation of this strange mound. Until he had seen the smoke rising from its summit, he had believed it to be merely a growth of tall forest trees surrounded by lesser trees and bushes that grew smaller as they neared the water. This is a common feature of that level Southern country, where the outer lines of vegetation are stunted by the constant high winds. Behind their protection, the inner circles of trees rise higher and higher until they attain a maximum size, and present an appearance of hills and mounds that proves most deceptive to strangers. The character of the smoke rising from the summit of this one had proved it to be something more than one of these ordinary tree mounds. Consequently the explorers were not surprised, after making their toilsome way through a forest of trees bound together with luxuriant vines, and brilliant with the blossoms of flowering air-plants, to find a veritable hill of earth rising before them. The forest encircled it, but ended at its base, and its sides were clothed only with a low growth of shrubs. They had hardly begun the ascent when they ran across a narrow but well-worn path leading to the summit.

On reaching the top they were disappointed to find it as lonely and unoccupied as the forest through which they had just passed. What they did find was a small cleared space from which even the grass had been worn away, and in the centre of which stood a sort of an altar of rough stones. It was about six feet square by four high, and was built of the ordinary coralline rock of the 'Glades. From this, or near it, the smoke must have ascended; but they looked in vain for ashes or other traces of a recent fire. The appearance of the altar showed that fires had been built on it; but there was nothing to indicate that one had burned there within an hour, and the mystery of the smoke became greater than ever.

If they had only been familiar with the Seminole method of making signal smokes, they would not have been so puzzled. A bright blaze of dry grass is smothered for an instant by a thick branch of green leaves. This is lifted and dropped again as often as the operator wishes to make a puff of smoke. Then the grass is allowed to burn out, and the wind, quickly dispersing the light ashes, removes every trace of the fire.

While disappointed and puzzled at finding no remnants of the fire that they were certain had recently burned there, nor of those who had lighted it, the explorers were enchanted with the beauty of the scene outspread on all sides of them. To the west the sun was sinking in wonderful glory behind the distant belt of cypress forest. Everywhere else the brown 'Glades, dotted with blue islands, seamed with the green threads of interlacing channels, and flashing with bits of open water, stretched beyond the limits of their vision. Over them hung a tremulous golden haze in which all objects were magnified and glorified. The all-pervading silence was only broken by the occasional rush on heavy pinions of flocks of snow-white ibises home-returning from their distant fishing-grounds.

"No wonder the Seminoles love this country, and dread the very thought of leaving it," said

Sumner, at length breaking the silence in which they had gazed on the exquisite scene.

"Yes, no wonder," replied the Lieutenant; "for in all my travels I don't know that I have ever seen anything more beautiful. But the most interesting of it all to me," he continued, "is this mound. It is evidently a structure of human erection, and must be contemporaneous with the famous earth pyramids of Mexico. Perhaps it was raised by the same wonderful prehistoric race. I have examined many of the well-known shell mounds of Florida, including those of Cedar Keys, and from there at various places down the west coast. I have also seen the great Turtle Mound on the Atlantic side, and those on the St. John's River; but all of them were evidently feast mounds, and showed in themselves the reason for their existence. I have heard of the earth mounds and ancient canals of the upper Caloosahatchie and Fish-eating Creek, but I have never heard it even intimated that similar structures might be looked for in the Everglades. Consequently I regard this one in the light of an important discovery. It is certainly sufficiently so to warrant us in spending to-morrow on this island investigating the mound as thoroughly as our means will allow."

"Doesn't that altar look as though the mound

had been used as a place for offering sacrifices?" asked Sumner.

"No; that altar, as you call it, is evidently of recent construction, and was probably built by the Indians now inhabiting this country as a place from which to make signal smokes, or possibly as a sepulchre. We will try to find out which to-morrow. These mounds were undoubtedly erected as places easy of defence, and perhaps this one may yield us some ancient weapons, as the 'kitchen middens,' or feast mounds, of Cedar Keys have so abundantly. I have seen quantities of celts and other stone implements taken from them, while the most exquisite quartz spear-head I ever saw was taken from a Caloosahatchie mound, which from descriptions must be very similar to this one. Oh yes, we certainly must spend another day on this island. Now we'd better be going, for it will soon be dark, and—"

Here the Lieutenant was interrupted by two shots fired in quick succession from the direction in which they had left Worth and Quorum.

"I am afraid that means trouble of some kind," said Lieutenant Carey, anxiously, after he had fired two answering shots.

Hurrying down the pathway, which they found led to the water on the opposite side of the island from that on which they had landed, they plunged into the forest, and were surprised to notice how dark it had already grown. Its intricacies were so bewildering and its difficulties so numerous that it was nearly an hour after they heard the shots before they came within sound of a voice answering their repeated calls.

At length they reached the place where they had left the boats, and here they found Worth alone, and so panic-stricken that it was with difficulty he could answer their eager questions.

"Why had he fired those shots?"

"Where was Quorum?"

"Where were the boats?"

"I fired them to call you back," answered the boy, "and I don't know where Quorum is nor where the boats are. They were here when I left, and when I came back they were gone. This was all I found here." With this Worth pointed to a bag of hardtack that lay on the ground at his feet. "And I'm afraid poor Quorum has been killed, for I know he never would have left us. I thought perhaps you were killed too, and that I was left here all alone, and I've been getting more and more frightened, until I think I should have gone crazy if you had not come when you did."

"You poor boy!" said the Lieutenant, soothingly, "I don't wonder that you were frightened. I should have been myself. But how did you happen to leave Quorum? and what was he doing when you left him?"

"He was sitting in the cruiser, and I only left him for a minute, because I heard such a big turkey gobbler right here in the woods close to us. I thought it would be such a pleasant surprise for you to have me get him for supper, and I was sure there weren't any panthers or rattlesnakes here. So I just crept into the bushes to get a shot at him, and he kept going farther and farther off, and I kept following him. I didn't see him at all, and after a while I didn't hear him any more either, so I thought I'd better come back. When I got here, I couldn't find Quorum or the boats, so I fired my gun as a signal."

"And you haven't seen nor heard anything of Quorum since?" inquired Lieutenant Carey, looking puzzled and anxious.

"No, I haven't heard a sound nor seen a sign of a living thing," answered Worth.

"There can't be any doubt of this being the right place," said the Lieutenant, reflectively, "for there is where we cut our way through the bushes."

"And here is the bag of biscuit," added Worth.

"I am not a bit surprised at the disappearance of the canoes," said Sumner. "I am getting used to that. But to have Quorum and the cruiser go too is certainly very strange."

"And leaves us in a most awkward predicament," added the Lieutenant. "If Quorum had only gone with one boat, we might expect to see him back at any moment; but to have them all go looks very suspicious. I greatly fear the poor fellow has been the victim of some foul play. However, it is too dark now to do anything but light a fire and prepare to pass the night where we are as well as we can under the circumstances."

Chapter XXVIII.

WHAT BECAME OF QUORUM AND THE CANOES.

When Worth and Quorum were left alone they sat for some time discussing the mystery of the smoke, and whether or not they had better begin unloading the boats and preparing camp. Worth advised against this. He hoped the others would discover a better camping-place than that. He also thought that perhaps they might return with news that would necessitate their leaving the island in a hurry. As he complained of being very hungry, Quorum got out the biscuit-bag, and they each took a hardtack from it. It was while they were eating these that the sound of a loud "gobble, gobble, gobble," came from the bushes, apparently but a few rods from where they sat.

Worth's hunting instinct was at once aroused, and slipping a couple of shells into his gun, he whispered: "You sit still, Quorum, and I'll have that fellow in a minute. My! but he must be a big one!"

Then he stepped noiselessly to the shore, and silently disappeared among the trees. Quorum sat with his back to the water, watching the spot where his young companion had entered the forest, and listening eagerly for the expected shot.

All at once a slight jar of the boat caused him to start; but before he could turn his head it was enveloped in a thick fold of cloth that effectually prevented his seeing or calling out. In a few seconds two active forms had bound his hands and feet, and slid him into the bottom of the boat, where he lay blinded, helpless, and nearly smothered. One of his captors picked up the biscuit-bag from which the prisoner had just been eating, and tossed it ashore with a low laugh.

In the mean time two others had been unfastening the canoes, and dragging them cautiously backward through the opening cut in the bushes to the channel, where lay the craft in which they had come. It was a large and well-shaped cypress dugout, capable of holding a dozen men. In less than three minutes from the time of Quorum's capture it was being poled rapidly but silently along through the twilight shadows, with the stolen boats in tow.

At a point about half a mile from the island these were skilfully concealed in a clump of tall grasses, and Quorum was bundled into the dugout. A choking sound from beneath the cloth that enveloped his head caused one of the strange canoemen to loosen it somewhat, so as to facilitate the prisoner's breathing. Then, propelled by four pairs of lusty young arms, the dugout shot away up one of the watery lanes leading directly into the heart of the 'Glades.

An hour later it was run ashore on one of the numerous islands whose purple outlines had so charmed the observers from the top of the mound. Here it was greeted by the barking of dogs and the sound of many voices. The thongs that bound Quorum's legs were cut, he was lifted to his feet, and, led by two of his captors, he was made to walk for some distance. At length he was halted, his wrists were unbound, and the cloth that enveloped his head was snatched from it.

The bewildered negro was instantly confronted by such a glare of firelight that for a minute his eyes refused to perform their duty. As he stood clumsily rubbing them, he heard a titter of laughter and the subdued sound of talking. As his eyes gradually became accustomed to the light, he saw, first, a fire directly in front of him, then, several palmetto huts, and at length a dozen or more Indian men, besides women and children, grouped in front of the huts, and all staring at him.

Until that moment he had not known who had

made him prisoner, nor why he had been carried off; and even now the second part of the question remained as great a mystery as ever. There was no doubt, however, that, for some purpose or other, he had been captured by a scouting party of Seminoles, and though Quorum had met individuals of this tribe while cruising on the reef, he had never visited one of their camps nor been in their power. He therefore gazed about him with considerable trepidation, and wondered what was going to be done with him.

As he did not recognize any of the dusky faces gathered in the firelight, he was amazed when one of the men, addressing him in broken English, said:

"How, Quor'm! How! Injun heap glad you come. You hongry? Eat sofkee. Good, plenty."

At the same time the speaker pointed to a smoking kettle of something that a squaw had just lifted from the fire and set close to the negro. A great wooden spoon was thrust into it, and its odor was most appetizing. Having fasted since early morning, Quorum was very hungry. Not only this, but under the circumstances he would have eaten almost anything his entertainers chose to set before him rather than run the risk of offending them. Therefore, without waiting for a second invitation, he squatted beside the kettle of sofkee, and began sampling its contents with the huge spoon. To his surprise, he had never in his life tasted a more delicious stew. After the first mouthful, he had no hesitation in eating such a meal as made even the Indians, among whom a large eater is considered worthy of respect, regard him with envious admiration.

It is no wonder that Quorum found this Indian food palatable, for the Seminole squaws are notable cooks, and sofkee is the tribal dish. It is a stew of venison, turtle, or some other meat, potatoes, corn, beans, peppers, and almost anything else that is at hand. It is thickened with coontie starch, and a kettleful of it is always to be found over one of the village fires, at the disposal of every hungry comer. The one drawback to its perfect enjoyment, according to a white man's fastidious taste, is that, besides the sofkee, the wooden spoon with which it is eaten is equally at the disposal of all comers, and is in almost constant use. This fact was not known to Quorum at the time of his introduction to sofkee. If it had been, it would hardly have lessened his relish of the meal, for Quorum was too wise to be fastidious.

He was so refreshed by his supper, as well as emboldened by the fact that no one seemed inclined to harm him, that something of his natural aggressiveness returned. After laying the sofkee spoon down, he turned to the Indian who had already spoken to him, and said:

"Why fo' yo' call me Quor'm? I 'ain't hab no 'quaintance wif you."

For answer the Indian only said, "Tobac, you got um, Quor'm?"

"Yes, sah. Tobac? I got er plenty ob him back yonder in de boat wha' yo' tuk me frum. Why fo' yo' treat a 'spectable colored gen'l'man dish yer way, anyhow? Wha' yo' mean by playin' sich tricks on him, an' on de white mans wha' trabblin' in he comp'ny?"

While speaking the negro had mechanically produced his black pipe, and instead of answering his questions, the Indian said: "Tobac. You no got um. Me got um, plenty. You take um, smoke um, bimeby talk heap."

With this he handed a plug of tobacco to the negro, who understood the action, if he had not fully comprehended the words that accompanied it. As he cut off a pipeful and carefully crumbled it in his fingers, he began to think that his position was not such a very unpleasant one, after all. He only wished he could imagine his fellow explorers as being half so comfortable as he was at that moment. Realizing from the Indian's last remark that there would be no talk until after the smoke, he assumed as comfortable a position as possible, and gazed curiously about him.

The little village, or camp, of half a dozen huts, was nearly hidden in the black shadows of the forest trees that surrounded it on all sides. Its huts were built of poles, supporting roofs of palmetto thatch, and were open at the sides. Each was provided with a raised floor of split poles, thickly covered with skins, and every hut contained one or more cheese-cloth sleeping canopies. Each hut had also several rifles and other hunting gear hanging in it, while canoe-masts, sails, paddles, and push poles leaned against its walls.

The men, who lay smoking on the furs inside the huts, or stretched in comfortable attitudes on the ground outside, were tall, clean-limbed, athletic-looking fellows clad in turbans of bright colors, gay calico shirts, and moccasins of deerskin; the women wore immense necklaces of beads, calico jackets, and long skirts, but were barefooted and bareheaded; and the children were clad precisely like their elders, with the exception of the turbans, which are denied to the boys and young men until they reach the age of warriors. Besides the Indians, Quorum saw that the camp was occupied by numbers of fowls, dogs, and small black pigs, that roamed through it at will. Everybody and everything in it, animals as well as humans, looked contented and well fed.

At length Quorum's smoke was finished, and he knocked the ashes from his pipe. As if this were a signal, the Indian men laid aside their pipes, and it was evident that the time for talking had arrived.

Chapter XXIX.

A VERY SERIOUS PREDICAMENT.

THE four explorers left on the mound island were very far from spending so pleasant an evening as that enjoyed by Quorum in the Seminole village. They were full of anxiety both as to his fate and their own. In some respects their position was not so bad as if they had been cast away on a desert island in the ocean, while in others it was worse. In the latter case they might hope to sight and signal some passing vessel, but here there was no chance for anything of that kind. At the best, they would not see anything except Indian canoes, and, under the circumstances, they could have little hope of obtaining aid from these.

Their revolvers were still loaded, and they had between them half a dozen cartridges for their guns, but thus far they had discovered no traces of game on the island. They would not lack for fresh-water, but with only a single bag of biscuit, the food question was likely to become a serious one within a short time. They had no knowledge of any white settlements within less than a hundred miles of where they were. These could only be reached by wading and swimming through the trackless 'Glades and bewildering cypress swamps. Undoubtedly some of the 'Glade islands were occupied by Indians, but they might explore as many of these as their strength would permit them to reach without finding one thus inhabited. Their situation was certainly a most perplexing one, and as they sat around a fire, eating a scanty supper of hardtack and discussing their prospects, these appeared gloomy in the extreme.

Still, the Lieutenant well knew that he must, if possible, keep up the spirits of his little party, and that the worst thing they could do was to take a hopeless view of the situation. So he said :

"Well, boys, though we seem to be in a nasty predicament, it might be a great deal worse, and we have still many things to be thankful for. I once drifted for a week in an open boat in the middle of the South Pacific. There were seven of us, and only one man of the party had the faith and courage to continue cheerful and hopeful through it all. On the very day that we swallowed our last drop of water, and while the rest of us were lying despairingly in the bottom of the boat, he sat up on watch, and finally discovered the trading schooner that picked us up."

"I," said Sumner, "do not feel nearly so badly now as I did when drifting out to sea in the dark on that wretched raft a couple of weeks ago. I expected every minute to be washed off and be snapped up by sharks; but, after all, the loneliness was the worst part of it."

"Right you are, Mr. Sumner," said the sailor. "A man can stand a heap of suffering along with others, that would throw him on his beam ends in no time if he was compelled to navigate by himself. I mind one time that I was lost in a fog, in a dory, on the Grand Banks. As we had grub and water in the boat, I didn't worry much, till my dorymate fell overboard and got drownded. The weight of his 'ilers and rubber boots sunk him like a shot. After that I wellnigh went crazy with the loneliness. I couldn't seem to eat or drink; and though I was picked up the very next day, that one night of loneliness seemed like a year of torment. Oh yes, sir, men can save themselves in company, when they won't lift a hand if left alone."

"I don't think I was ever in a worse fix than this one," remarked Worth, dolefully.

"Probably not, my boy," said the Lieutenant,

cheerily. "You are young yet, and have just made a start on your career of adventure. All things must have a beginning, you know. The next time you find yourself in an unpleasant situation, you will take great satisfaction in looking back and describing this one as having been much worse. No adventure worth the telling can be had without a certain degree of mental or physical suffering, and the more of this that is endured the greater the satisfaction in looking back on it. Now that we can do nothing before daylight, I propose that we make ourselves as comfortable as possible, and sleep as soundly as possible. By so doing we shall be able to face our situation with renewed strength and courage in the morning. To-morrow we will explore the island, discover its resources, and perhaps find traces of Quorum and the boats. Failing in this, I propose that we construct as good a raft as we can with the means at hand. With it to carry our guns, besides affording us some support, we will make our way back to the place where those cowboys were camped this morning. From there we can follow their trail until we overtake them, or reach some settlement."

Cheered by having a definite plan of operations thus outlined, all hands set to work to gather such materials for bedding as they could find in the darkness, and an hour later the little camp was buried in profound slumber.

To their breakfast of hardtack the following morning Sumner added a hatful of cocoa-plums that he had gathered while the others still slept. Soon after sunrise they divided into two parties — the Lieutenant and Worth forming one, and Sumner and the sailor the other—and set out in opposite directions to make their way around the island.

"I don't want any one to fire a gun except in case of absolute necessity," said Lieutenant Carey. "And if a shot is heard from either party, the others will at once hasten in that direction."

"Can't we even shoot my gobbler if we meet him?" queried Worth.

"No, I think not," replied the Lieutenant, with a smile; "that is, unless he shows fight, for I expect your gobbler would turn out to be a turkey without feathers, and standing about six feet high. I mean," he added, as Worth's puzzled face showed that he did not understand, "that the call by which you were led away from Quorum was, in all likelihood, uttered by an Indian for that very purpose."

So difficult was their progress through the luxuriant and densely-matted undergrowth of that

Everglade isle that, though it was not more than a couple of miles in circumference, it was nearly noon before the two parties again met. They had discovered nothing except that the island was uninhabited, and they were its sole occupants. Nor had they seen anything that would give a clew to the fate that had overtaken poor Quorum.

"While I don't for a moment suppose that the fellow has deserted," said the Lieutenant, "I wish, with all my heart, that we knew what had become of him."

"Indeed, he has not deserted," replied Sumner, warmly. "I'll answer for Quorum as I would for myself. Wherever he is, he will come back to us if he gets half a chance."

"Yes, I believe he will; and I only hope he may get the chance. Now let us go to the top of the mound for one more comprehensive look at our surroundings, and then we will begin our preparations for leaving the island."

From the summit of the mound the same tranquil scene on which Lieutenant Carey and Sumner had gazed with such pleasure the evening before, only more widely extended, greeted their eyes. It was as devoid of human life now as then, and its present beauties failed to interest them.

"I said that we would probably spend to-day here," remarked the Lieutenant. "But I must confess that my present interest in this mound lies in getting away from it as quickly as possible. I have no longer the least desire to investigate its mysteries, and so let us descend to our more important work."

Returning to their landing-place, and eating a most unsatisfactory lunch of hardtack, they began to search for materials from which to build their raft. These were hard to find, and still harder to prepare for the required purpose. There was plenty of timber, but it was green, and they had no weapons with which to attack it except their sheath-knives. Neither had they any nails nor ropes, and their lashings must be made of vines.

After a whole afternoon of diligent labor, a nondescript affair of different lengths and jagged ends lay on the ground at the water's edge ready for launching. With infinite difficulty and pains they got it into the water, only to have the mortification of seeing it immediately sink.

"Well, boys," said the Lieutenant, in a voice that trembled in spite of his effort to make it sound cheerful, "that raft is a decided failure. Unless we can find some wood better suited to our purpose, I am afraid we must give up the idea altogether, and try to reach the cypress belt without any such aid."

"If we only had a few sticks of the timber that is so plenty along the reef!" said Sumner, thinking of his own previous efforts in the raft line.

"We might as well wish for our canoes, and done with it," said Worth, despondently.

Just then they thought they heard a far-away shout in the forest behind them. Instinctively grasping their guns, they stood in listening attitudes. It was repeated, this time more distinctly, and they looked at each other wonderingly.

At the third shout Sumner exclaimed, joyously: "It's Quorum! I know it is!" He would have plunged into the forest to meet the newcomer, but the Lieutenant restrained him, saying: "Wait a minute. Let us be sure that this is not another trap."

A few moments later there was no longer any mistaking the voice, and their answering shouts guided Quorum, his honest face beaming with joy and excitement, to the place where they were awaiting him.

Chapter XXX.

QUORUM AS AN AMBASSADOR.

It was Quorum, sure enough, not only alive and well, but seemingly in the best of spirits. Where had he been? Where were the boats? How did he get back? and where had he come from? These are only samples of the dozens of questions with which he was plied while shaking hands with his friends, including the Lieutenant, who was as heartily rejoiced as the boys at again seeing the faithful fellow.

At one of the questions thus asked him, Quorum's face fell, and he answered:

"Whar de boats is, honey, I don't know, fer I hain't seen no likeness ob dem sence las' night 'bout dis time. Whar I is bin, an' what I is 'sperienced, is er long story; but hit's got ter be tole right now, kase dat's what I hyar fer. What we do nex' depen' on de way you all take hit when I is done tellin'."

Then they sat down, and forgetful of their hunger, their recent disappointment with the raft, and even of their unhappy predicament, the others listened with absorbed interest to Quorum's story.

He described the way in which he had been carried off, and his reception in the Indian camp.

"They were Indians, then?" interrupted the Lieutenant.

"Yes, sah, shuah 'nough Injuns, an' a powerful sight ob dem—man, squaw, an' pickaninny, an' dey gib ole Quor'm one ob de fines' suppahs he ebber eat."

"I wish we had one like it here at this minute!" said Sumner, thus reminded of his hunger.

"Den we all smoke de peace-pipe, so dey don't hab no fear ob me declarin' er war on 'em," continued Quorum.

"Them Injuns has got tobacco, then?" queried the sailor, whose smoking outfit had disappeared with the boats.

"Ob cose dey is, er plenty," answered Quorum. "An' den me an' de big chiefs sot down fer what yo' might call a considerashun ob de fac's. Dey say as what dey can't noways 'low dis hyer experdishun to pass troo de 'Glades, 'cep' on condishuns."

Told in more intelligible language than that used by Quorum, the substance of his talk with the Indians was as follows:

They had learned from a white man that the objects of Lieutenant Carey's expedition were to spy out their land, discover their numbers and the value of their property, and make preparations for their removal from that part of the country.

"I hope you told them differently, and explained our real objects," said the Lieutenant.

"Yes, sah; I done tell 'em to de full ob my knowingness ob yo' plans. But seein' as I hain't know nuffin' tall 'bout 'em, maybe I don't make hit berry cl'ar ter dem igerant sabages; but I done hit as well as I know how."

The Indians had declared that they should resist any such attempt at an investigation of their resources and mode of life, and that the party must turn back from where it now was. If it would do so, its boats should be restored, and it would be allowed to depart in peace.

The difficulties in the way of accepting this proposition had at once been seen by Quorum. He had explained that as their small boats were not fitted to cruise in the open waters of the Gulf, and as their big boat was already on its way to the east coast, where they were to meet it, to turn back would be a great hardship.

The Indians had listened gravely to their interpreter's translation of all that he had to say on the subject, and assented to the force of his arguments. Then they proposed another plan. It was that if the whites would give up their arms and trust entirely to them, they would convey the party and their boats safely across the 'Glades to within a short distance of the east coast. There they should again receive their guns, and should be allowed to depart in peace, provided they would promise not to return.

"Seems to me that is quite a liberal proposition," said the Lieutenant, after Quorum had succeeded in making it clearly understood. "All we want is to cross the 'Glades and see the Indians. I would willingly have paid them to guide us, and now they offer to do so of their own accord. I can't conceive how you persuaded them to make such an offer, Quorum. You must be a born diplomat."

"Yes, sah," replied the negro, grinning from ear to ear, "I 'specs I is." At the same time he had no more idea of what the Lieutenant meant than if he had talked in Greek.

"How does that plan strike you, boys?" asked Lieutenant Carey, turning to Sumner and Worth.

"It strikes me as almost too good to be true," answered the former. "And I'm afraid there's some trick behind it all; but then I don't see what we can do except say yes to almost any offer they may choose to make."

"That is so," said the Lieutenant. "Without our boats, and with no means for making a raft, we are about as helpless as we well can be."

"It seems to me a splendid plan," said Worth, who saw visions of peaceful nights, and days pleasantly spent in hunting and in visiting Indian camps.

Although the sailor's opinion had not been asked, he could not help remarking: "I'm agin trusting an' Injin, sir. Injins and Malays and all them sort of niggers are notoriously deceitful."

"Hi! Wha' yo' say dere 'bout niggahs, yo' sailorman?" exclaimed Quorum, in high dudgeon. "Yo' call 'em notorious, eh?"

"Not black ones," answered the sailor, apologetically—"not black ones, Quorum; but them as is red and yellow."

"Dat's all right, sah, an' I 'cept yo' 'pology. At de same time I is bankin' on de squar'ness ob dem Injuns who I bin councillin' wif."

"You believe it will be safe to trust them, then?" asked the Lieutenant.

"Yes, sah; yo' kin trus' 'em same like a black man."

"Very well," said Lieutenant Carey; "as I

don't see how, in the present state of affairs, we can do anything else, I will take your word for their honesty, and accept their conditions; only I will not promise never to come into the 'Glades again. I will only promise not to turn directly back from the east coast after they have left us."

"Dat's wha' dey mean, sah. I is berry 'tic'lar on dat pint ob de controbersy."

"Then we will consider it as settled, and would like to leave here for a place where there is something to eat as quickly as possible. Where are your Indian friends?"

"Out dere, sah, in de cooners. Dey say when yo' ready, den I holler like er squinch-owl, an' brung down all yo' uns' guns an' resolvers de fustes' t'ing."

"Very well, squinch away then, and here are my pistols. It is certainly humiliating to be disarmed to please a lot of Indians; but hunger and necessity are such powerful persuaders that it is best to submit to them with as good grace as possible."

So Quorum "squinched" in a manner that no self-respecting owl would have recognized; but which answered the purpose so well that an answer was immediately heard from the water, over which the evening shadows were now fast falling.

Directly afterwards a canoe, containing the

Indian who had acted as interpreter during Quorum's council with the chiefs, appeared at the opening in the bushes. Without stepping ashore, this Indian, whose name was Ul-we (the tall one), exchanged a few words with Quorum, whereby he learned that the Seminole conditions were accepted by the white men. He then bade the negro place the guns and pistols in the canoe and enter it himself. Then he shoved off, and another canoe, containing two Indians, made its appearance.

The Lieutenant bade Sumner and Worth step into it first; but the moment they had done so, it too was shoved off, and another canoe, also containing two Indians, appeared in its place. This received the Lieutenant and the sailor. By the time it was poled into the channel the foremost canoe had disappeared in the darkness, nor was it again seen.

During their journey both the Lieutenant and Sumner tried to enter into conversation with the Indians in their respective canoes, but after a few futile attempts they gave it up. To all their questions they received the same answer, which was "Un-cah" (Yes), and not another word could the Indians be persuaded to utter.

The Lieutenant consoled himself with the thought that he would be able to talk to the

chiefs through the interpreter; while the boys looked forward with eager anticipations to seeing the Indian village that Quorum had described. As for the sailor, Indians and their villages were matters of indifference to him. What he looked forward to was a good supper and a pipe of tobacco.

Thus, all of them awaited with impatience their journey's end, and wished it were light enough for them to see whither they were being taken.

Chapter XXXI.

A CLOSELY GUARDED CAMP.

The darkness, which comes so quickly after sunset in that far Southern country, with almost no intervening twilight, effectually prevented our explorers from seeing where they were going. They only knew from the stars that their general direction was east, or directly into the heart of the Everglades. They were even unable to study the countenances, dress, or general appearance of the young Indians who, standing in the bow and stern of each canoe, drove it forward with unerring judgment and at a considerable speed by means of long push poles. These poles were quite slender; but each terminated at its lower end in an enlargement, formed by fastening a short bit of wood to either side that prevented it from sinking deeply into the sand or grass roots against which it was set.

The canoes in which our voyagers were now travelling were as different from their own dainty craft as one boat can be from another. Nor did they bear the least resemblance to the bark canoes of Northern Indians, there being no Southern bark similar to that of the Northern birch, or suitable for canoe-building. They were simply dugouts, from twenty to twenty-five feet long by about three feet broad, hollowed with great skill from huge cypress logs. Their lines were fine, and, as our friends afterwards discovered, they are capital sailing craft in any wind, except dead ahead.

When a Seminole decides to build one of these canoes, he first selects and fells his tree, cutting off a section of the required length, and free from knots or cracks. The upper surface of this is hewn smooth, with a slight sheer rise fore and aft. On this smooth surface a plan of the canoe is carefully outlined with charcoal, and then the outside is laboriously worked into shape with hatchets. The hollowing out of the inside is accomplished by fire and hatchets, and, considering the limited supply of tools at the builders' disposal, the result is a triumph of marine architecture. Hatchets and knives are the only tools used in the making of the masts, spars, paddles, push poles, and spear handles that are needed for the equipment of each canoe. The ingenious builders also cut and sew their own sails, which they make of unbleached muslin bought from the trader on Biscayne Bay. Although they use no keels, centre-boards, nor lee-boards, they manage by holding their paddles firmly against the side of the canoe and deep in the water to sail close-hauled, and to keep her up to the wind in a manner that is truly surprising. The Indians take great pride in their canoes and value them highly, for, as they are without horses, roads, or any considerable area of dry land, these are their sole means of transportation and communication between the different parts of the vast territory over which they roam.

After travelling several miles, this first voyage of our explorers in Indian canoes ended at a heavily wooded islet, between the trees of which they could see the welcome glow of a camp-fire. To their great delight, as they reached the shore, they found their own canoes and the cruiser safely moored to it. In spite of their joy at again seeing these, they were too hungry and too impatient to visit the Indian village to do more just then than assure themselves that their own boats were all right. Then they hurried towards the fire.

There was a roomy palmetto hut standing near it; but to their surprise the firelight disclosed only a single human figure, which, as they drew near, proved to be that of Quorum. He was hard at work cooking supper, and only acknowledged their presence with a grin, and the announcement that it would be ready in a few minutes.

Turning to the hut, they saw that it had been recently erected, and that it contained their own rolls of bedding, besides the little bags of toilet articles belonging to Lieutenant Carey and the boys, which Quorum had thoughtfully taken from the canoes and placed ready for their use.

"I never realized the luxury of brushes and combs before!" exclaimed Worth, as he occupied the time before supper with making what was probably the most elaborate toilet ever seen in the Everglades.

Meanwhile the Lieutenant was questioning Quorum as to the location of the Indian village, and was disappointed to find the negro as ignorant on the subject as himself. Quorum thought it must be on some other island, as this certainly was not the place to which he had been taken the night before. He said that on arriving there he had found the canoes and cruiser, the hut built, and the fire lighted. The young Indian who had brought him had helped carry the things up to the hut, and also given him some venison and vegetables in exchange for a small quantity of coffee and sugar. He had remained there until shortly before the arrival of the others, and Quorum had not noticed when he disappeared. Before leaving, he had told Quorum that, by the chief's orders, the white men would remain on that island until the following evening.

"Oh, we will, will we?" said Lieutenant Carey, whose pride chafed against receiving orders from an Indian, even if he was a chief. "With our own boats at hand, I don't see what is to hinder us from leaving when we please. I wish that chief would hurry up and put in an appearance. I want to have a few words with him."

He now for the first time realized that the young Indians who had brought them there had not followed them to the camp, and he stepped down to the water's edge to see what they were doing. To his dismay he found that they had not only disappeared, but had taken the canoes and cruiser with them. Greatly provoked at this, he returned to the camp in a very unpleasant frame of mind, mentally abusing the Indians, and regretting that, by accepting their conditions, he had so completely placed himself in their power. His good-nature was somewhat restored by the supper, which was most bountiful and well cooked, and by the soothing pipe smoke that followed it; for among other things, Quorum had not neglected to bring up a plentiful supply of tobacco.

After supper, as he and the boys lay out-stretched on their blankets within the hut, the open side of which faced the fire, the Lieutenant acknowledged that their present position was a vast improvement on that of the night before. The boys agreed with him, though at the same time they were even more disappointed than he at not finding themselves in an Indian village. That was one of the things they had most counted on seeing in the Everglades. Having finally decided to make the best of their situation, and to obtain the greatest possible amount of comfort and pleasure from it, they turned in, and slept soundly until morning.

They were so thoroughly tired with their various hardships and labors of the two preceding days and nights that they slept late, and the sun had already been up for several hours before they answered the negro's call to breakfast. He said that though he had been down to the shore several times after water, he had seen no signs of either canoes or Indians. Thus to all appearances they were not only the sole occupants of the island, but of the 'Glades as well.

As they had nothing else to do, the Lieutenant proposed to the boys that they should explore this new island, and make such discoveries of other islands and the intervening 'Glades as could be seen from its shores. They readily agreed to this, and the three set forth. They had not gone more than a hundred yards from camp when they were suddenly confronted by a young Indian, armed with a rifle, which he pointed at them, at the same time making other signs to them to go back. At first they were greatly startled by his unexpected appearance. Then the Lieutenant undertook to remonstrate with him, and to explain that they only wanted to walk harmlessly about and view the landscape, but all in vain. The stolid-faced young savage either could not or would not understand. He only shook his head without uttering a word, but continued to make signs for them to go back.

"This is one of the strangest and most irritating things that I ever heard of!" exclaimed Lieutenant Carey, after finding his efforts to communicate with the Indian unavailing. "If we only had our guns, I'd make that fellow let us pass or know the reason why. As we haven't any, and he has one, the argument is too one-sided, and we might as well retire from it as gracefully as possible. Let us try another direction, and find out if that is also guarded." They tried in two other places, only to be repulsed by other determined young guards who, mute as statues, were equally stolid and impervious to argument.

"THEY WERE SUDDENLY CONFRONTED BY AN INDIAN ARMED WITH A RIFLE."

There was nothing to do but to return to the hut and make the best of the situation. From there no signs of an Indian was to be seen; but let one of the inmates of the camp stroll beyond its limits in any direction, and the woods seemed to swarm with them, though the guards probably did not number more than half a dozen in all.

The day was passed in eating, sleeping, and in discussing their peculiar situation. They were evidently prisoners, though to all appearances as free as air; but, as Lieutenant Carey said, there was no chance of their escaping from the island anyhow, so why they should be denied the privilege of walking about it he could not understand. Quorum was equally in the dark with the rest, and said that nothing of the kind had been intimated by the chiefs during their talk with him. It was finally decided that instead of being on a small island as they had supposed, they must be at one end of a large one that contained a village at the other, which, for some unknown reason, the Indians did not choose they should visit. With this solution of the problem they were forced to content themselves, and they waited with impatience the coming of night, when, according to what Ul-we had told Quorum, their journey was to be resumed.

Chapter XXXII.

CROSSING THE 'GLADES WITHOUT SEEING THEM.

They had an early supper, so as to be all ready for a start whenever their jailers should see fit to make one. By sunset their blankets were rolled up, and they were impatiently awaiting some signal; but none came until darkness had fully set in. Then once more from the direction of the water came the now familiar cry of a screech-owl. It was answered from several points about the camp, which showed their Indian guards to be still on duty. As Quorum had been allowed to go freely to the shore for water during the day, the Lieutenant now told him to go down again and discover the meaning of the signal. He returned a minute later with the news that Ul-we was waiting for him and the cooking utensils, and that the canoes for the other passengers would arrive with the setting of the new moon, which hung low in the western sky.

So Quorum left them, as on the previous night. As the silver crescent of Halissee, the night timepiece of the Everglades, sank from sight, the others went to the shore, carrying their blankets with them. There they found two canoes, apparently manned by the same silent crews of the evening before, awaiting them.

As they shoved off and plunged once more into the trackless 'Glades, the Lieutenant turned for a look at the island. He could distinguish its black outlines from end to end, and it was a very small one. This overthrew the only theory they had formed concerning their close imprisonment, and left him more than ever puzzled as to its object.

Hour after hour the long poles were steadily wielded by the silent Indians, who seemed not to know fatigue nor to require rest. All through the night the heavy dugouts pursued their steady way, crashing through the crisp bonnets, and bending down the long grasses, that flew up with a "swish" behind them. It was a marvel to the passengers that the channels, followed as unerringly by the dusky canoemen as though it had been daylight, always led into one another. Their own experience had been that, even with sunlight to guide them, half the channels they had attempted to follow proved blind leads. But with the Indians it was never so.

Through the night Lieutenant Carey pondered his situation, and studied their course by the stars. These told him that it was a little to the north of east, the very one he would have chosen, and in this respect the situation was satisfactory. But what information was he gaining concerning the Everglades, their resources, and present population? About as little as was possible for one who was actually passing through them. Could he obtain any more? Evidently not, under the circumstances. Long and deeply as he pondered the subject, he could not think of a single feasible plan for altering the existing state of affairs. He was compelled to acknowledge himself completely outwitted by the simple-minded sons of the forest into whose power he had so curiously fallen. "If I could only get at them, and talk to them, and explain matters to them!" he said aloud; and the sailor answered:

"It wouldn't do no good, sir. There's none in the world so obstinate as Injins and Malays. Once they gets an idea inside their skulls, all the white talk you could give 'em wouldn't drive it out. Fighting is the only argument they can understand; and, if you say the word, I'll have these two heathen pitched overboard in no time."

"No," said the Lieutenant, "it wouldn't do any good, and my orders are to treat such Indians as I may meet with all possible friendliness. I only wish I could meet with some besides these two young automatons, but there does not seem to be any prospect of it."

At the same time Sumner and Worth, crouched snugly among their blankets in the bottom of the other canoe, were also talking of their strange situation.

"Do you suppose any other two fellows ever had such queer times on a canoe trip as we are having?" asked Worth.

"Indeed I do not," replied Sumner. "And this is the very queerest part of it. Here we are still on a canoe cruise, without our own canoes, without knowing where we are going, and without having anything to do with the management of the craft we are cruising in. It will be a queer experience to tell about when you get back to New York, won't it?"

"Yes, indeed, it will, though New York seems so very far away that it is hard to realize that I shall ever get there again. If we could only see an Indian village, though! It seems too bad to be going right through an Indian country and yet see nothing of its people."

"Oh, well, we are not through with the 'Glades yet, and you may still have a chance to see plenty of Indians."

In spite of Sumner's hopefulness, Worth's wish did not seem any nearer being gratified four days from that time than it did then. Each night's journey was a repetition of the first, except that they grew shorter with the growing moon. The Indians refused to travel except in darkness, and never came for their passengers until after the moon had set. Each day was spent in a comfortable camp, to which they were so closely confined that they could learn nothing of their surroundings. These camps were always located on small islands, and were always reached before daylight.

Quorum always arrived at the camping-place some time in advance of the others, and he always found the canoes and the cruiser awaiting him. From them he was allowed to take whatever he thought the party would need, but after that first night the boats invariably disappeared before the others reached them.

Sumner said this was a trick the canoes had learned early on the cruise, and they had probably taught it to the other boat.

Who caused their disappearance or where they went to, none of them knew; and but for Quorum the owners of the several craft would have heard nothing of their whereabouts or welfare.

During this strange journey, as they were unable to do any hunting or foraging for themselves, Quorum was obliged to exchange so many

A Story of the Everglades.

of their stores for fresh meat, fruit, and vegetables, that he finally announced them to be nearly exhausted.

At length, one very dark night, the passengers, who were half dozing in the bottoms of the canoes, became conscious of a change. The darkness all at once grew more intense, until they could barely distinguish the forms of the Indians in the bow and stern of their respective boats. A rank odor of decaying vegetation filled the air, while the swish of grass and bonnets was no longer heard. They seemed to be moving more swiftly and easily than usual. Finally, when they landed, it did not seem as though they were on an island; and as they made their way towards the light of the camp-fire, about which Quorum was already busy, they suddenly realized that it was reflected from a background of pine-trees.

"Hurrah, boys!" shouted Lieutenant Carey; "there is a sign that our trip is nearly ended. Pine-trees don't grow in the 'Glades, and therefore we must be somewhere near the coast. I can't say that I am sorry, for the trip has been a most disappointing one to me. It has been a decidedly unique and remarkable one, though— has it not? I wonder how many people will believe us when we say that we have crossed the entire width of the Everglades without learning anything about them, and almost without seeing them? When we add that we have passed dozens of Indian villages, and yet have not seen an Indian village; have been surrounded by Indians, but cannot describe their appearance; have come all the way by water, and brought our own boats with us, and yet have not set eyes on our own boats since the day we entered the 'Glades—I am afraid that we shall be regarded much as the old woman regarded her sailor son when he told her that he had seen fish with wings and able to fly. In fact, I am afraid they will doubt our veracity. How I am going to get up any kind of a report to send to Washington, I am sure I don't know. By-the-way, Quorum, were our canoes here when you landed?"

"No, sah, dey wasn't; an' I is troubled in my min' frum worryin' about dem. I is ask dat feller Ul-we, but he don't say nuffin.' 'Pears like he done los' he tongue, like de res' ob de Injuns. De wust ob hit is, sah, dat de grub jes about gin out, an' I is got er mighty pore 'pology fer a breakfus."

So excited were our explorers over their new surroundings, and over this report that their boats were again missing, that instead of turning in for a nap, as usual, they sat round the fire and waited impatiently for daylight. Sumner was the most uneasy of the party, and every few minutes he would get up and walk away from the firelight, the better to see if the day were not breaking.

On one of these occasions he was gone so much longer than usual that the others were beginning to wonder what had become of him. All at once they heard him shouting from the direction of the place at which they had landed:

"Hello! in the camp! Come down here, quick! I've got something to show you."

Chapter XXXIII.

AN ADVENTUROUS DEER-HUNT.

In answer to Sumner's call, the others sprang up and hurried in the direction of his voice. As they got beyond the circle of firelight they saw that the day was breaking, though in the forest its light was dim and uncertain. It was much stronger ahead of them, and within a minute they stood at the water's edge, where objects near at hand were plainly discernible. Although they more than suspected that the 'Glades had been left behind, they were hardly prepared for the sight that greeted their eyes. Instead of a limitless expanse of grass and water dotted with islands, they saw a broad river flowing dark and silently towards the coming dawn through a dense growth of tall forest trees. But for the direction of its current, it was a counterpart of the one, now so far behind, by which they had entered the 'Glades from the Gulf.

Of more immediate importance even than the river were the objects to which Sumner triumphantly directed their attention. These were the long-unseen canoes and the cruiser, with masts, sails, and paddles in their places, and looking but little the worse for their journey than when their owners had stepped from them nearly a week before. Sumner had discovered them, snugly moored to the bank, a short distance below the landing-place, and had towed them up to where the others now saw them. In the bottom of the *Hu-la-lah* lay their guns and pistols, carefully oiled and in perfect order. Everything was in place, and they could not find that a single article of their outfit was missing.

"I declare!" said the Lieutenant, "those Indians are decent fellows, after all, and though I am provoked with them for their obstinacy in not granting us a single interview, as well as for the way they compelled us to journey through their country, I can't help admiring the manner in which they have fulfilled their share of our contract. They have shown the utmost fairness and honesty in all their dealings with us, and I don't know that I blame them for the way in which they have acted. They have been treated so abominably by the Government ever since Florida came into our possession that they certainly have ample cause to be suspicious of all white men."

Quorum was sent down to watch the canoes

and see that they did not again disappear, while the others ate the scanty breakfast that he had prepared. At it they drank the last of their coffee, and Quorum reported that there was nothing left of their provisions save some corn-meal and a few biscuit.

As they talked of this state of affairs, Sumner said that he had started up a deer when he went after the canoes, and Worth was confident that this must be a good place in which to find his favorite game—wild turkeys.

"It looks as though we would have to stop here long enough to do a little hunting before proceeding any farther," said the Lieutenant.

To this proposition the boys, eager to use their recovered guns, readily agreed.

So, after making sure that their camp was no longer guarded, and that they were at liberty to go where they pleased, it was decided to devote the morning to hunting, with the hope of replenishing their larder. Quorum and the sailor were left to guard camp and the boats, while the others entered the piny woods, going directly back from the river. The Lieutenant carried a rifle and the boys their shot-guns, while each had his pockets well filled with loaded shells.

The pine forest was filled with a dense undergrowth of saw-palmetto, and the ground beneath these was covered with rough masses of broken coralline rock. It was also slippery with a thick coating of brown pine-needles. Under these circumstances, therefore, it was almost impossible to proceed silently, and whatever game they might have seen received ample warning of their approach in time to make good its escape.

When they at length came to a grassy savanna, on the opposite side of which was a small hammock of green, shrubby trees, the Lieutenant proposed that the boys remain concealed where they were while he made a long circuit around it. He would thus approach from its leeward side, and any game that he might scare up would be almost certain to come in their direction. After stationing them a few hundred feet apart, so that they could cover a greater territory, and warning them to keep perfectly quiet, he left them.

The sky was clouded, and a high wind soughed mournfully through the tops of the pines. Every now and then the boys were startled by the crash of a falling branch, while the grating of the interlocking limbs above them sounded like distressed moanings. It was all so dismal and lonesome that finally Worth could stand it no longer, and made his way to where Sumner was sitting.

"Have you noticed how full the air is of

smoke?" he said, as he approached his companion. "My eyes are smarting from it."

"Yes," replied Sumner, "it has given me a choking sensation for some time. I expect the woods are on fire somewhere."

"Really!" said Worth, looking about him, apprehensively. "Then don't you think we ought to be getting back towards the river?"

"No, not yet. The fire must be a long way off still, and it would never do for us to leave without Lieutenant Carey. He would think we were lost, and be terribly anxious. There he is now! Did you hear that?"

Yes, Worth heard the distant rifle-shot that announced the Lieutenant's whereabouts. Instantly his freshly aroused hunting instinct banished all thoughts of the fire, and he hurried back to his post. He had not more than reached it before there came a crashing among the palmettoes, and ere the startled boy realized its cause, two deer, bounding over the undergrowth with superb leaps, dashed past him and disappeared.

"Why didn't you fire?" cried Sumner, hurrying up a moment later. "It was a splendid shot! I would give anything for such a chance!"

"I never thought of it," answered Worth, ruefully. "Besides, they went so quickly that I didn't have time."

"They ought to have stood still for a minute or two, that's a fact," said Sumner, who was rather inclined to laugh at his less experienced companion.

Just then there came another crashing of the palmettoes, and a third deer bounded into sight for an instant, only to disappear immediately as the others had done.

"Why didn't you fire?" laughed Worth. "It was a splendid shot!"

"Because this is your station," replied Sumner, anxious to conceal beneath this weak excuse the fact that he had been fully as startled and unnerved as his companion. "I do believe, though," he added, "that this last fellow was wounded, and perhaps we may get him yet."

The discovery of fresh blood on the palmetto leaves through which the flying animal had passed confirmed this belief, and without a thought of the possible consequences the boys set off in hot pursuit of the wounded deer.

They easily followed the trail of the blood-smeared leaves, and in the ardor of their pursuit they might have gone a mile, or they might have gone ten for all they knew, when suddenly, without warning, they came face to face with the deer. He was a full-grown buck, with branching antlers still in the velvet, and by his swaying from side to side he was evidently exhausted. The sight of his enemies seemed to infuse him with renewed strength, and the next instant he charged fiercely towards them.

Worth, attempting to run, tripped and fell in his path. Sumner, with better luck, sprang aside, and sent a charge of buckshot into the furious animal at such short range that the muzzle of his gun nearly touched it. It fell in a heap on top of Worth, gave one or two convulsive kicks, and was dead.

Its warm life-blood spurted over the prostrate boy, and when Sumner dragged him from beneath the quivering carcass he was smeared with it from head to foot.

"Are you hurt, old man?" inquired Sumner, anxiously, as his companion leaned heavily on him, trembling from exhaustion and his recent fright.

"I don't know that I am," replied Worth, with a feeble attempt at a smile. "I expect I am only bruised and scratched. But, oh, Sumner, what an awfully ferocious thing a deer is! Seems to me they are as bad as panthers. What wouldn't I give for a drink of water! I can hardly speak, I am so choked with smoke."

With this, Sumner suddenly became aware that the smoke, which they had not noticed in the excitement of their chase, had so increased in density that breathing was becoming difficult. Thoroughly alarmed, he looked about him. In all directions the woods were full of it, and even at a short distance the trees showed indistinctly through its blue haze. Now, for the first time, the boys were conscious of a dull roar with which the air was filled. Their long chase must have led them directly towards the fire.

"We must get back to camp as quickly as possible!" exclaimed Sumner, realizing at once the danger of their situation. "Come on, Worth, we haven't a moment to lose!"

"But what shall we do with our deer?" asked the blood-covered boy, who could not bear the thought of relinquishing their hard-won prize.

"Never mind the deer, but come along!" replied Sumner. "If I am not mistaken, we shall have our hands full taking care of ourselves. That fire is coming down on us faster than we can run, and we haven't any too much start of it as it is."

Chapter XXXIV.

HEMMED IN BY A FOREST FIRE.

Which way were they to fly? The terrible roar of the burning forest seemed to come from all directions, and the smoke seemed hardly less dense on one side than on another. But there had been no fire where they came from, and they must retrace their steps along the blood-marked trail that they had followed, of course. Although the body of the deer lay near the spot where it had ended, they were at first too bewildered to discover it, and lost several precious minutes in searching among the palmetto leaves for its crimson signs. At length they found them, and started back on a run.

It was exhausting work trying to run through the thick scrub, over its loglike roots, and among the rough rock masses strewn in the wildest confusion between them, and their speed was quickly reduced to a walk. Sumner went ahead, and, with arms uplifted to protect his face from the sawlike edges of the stout leaf stems, forced a way through them, with Worth close behind him.

They had not gone far when Sumner suddenly stopped and, with a despairing gesture, pointed ahead. The flames were in front of them, and could be distinctly seen licking the brown tree trunks, and stretching their writhing arms high aloft towards the green tops.

"We are going right into the fire!" the boy exclaimed, hoarsely. "The deer must have seen it, and been curving away from it when we overtook him!"

So they turned back, and rushed blindly, without trying to follow the trail, in the opposite direction. Before they had gone half a mile Worth's strength became exhausted, and he sank down on a palmetto root gasping for breath.

"I can't go any farther, Sumner! Oh, I can't!" he cried, piteously.

"But you must! You can't stay here to be burned to death! We are almost certain to find a slough with water in it, or a stream!" and grasping his comrade by the arm, Sumner pulled him again to his feet.

As he did so, the hammers of Worth's gun became caught in something, and the next instant both barrels were discharged with a startling explosion.

"That's a good idea!" exclaimed Sumner. "Let's fire all our cartridges as fast as we can.

Perhaps they are out looking for us, and will hear the shots."

So saying, he fired both barrels of his own gun into the air, and quickly reloading, fired again. Worth followed suit; but just as Sumner was ready to fire for the third time he was startled by a sharp crackling sound close beside him. He turned quickly. There was a bright blaze within ten feet of him. The first accidental discharge of Worth's gun, as it lay pointed directly into a mass of dry grass and dead palmetto leaves, had set this on fire. Worth instinctively sprang towards it with the intention of trying to stamp it out, but, with a joyful cry, Sumner restrained him.

"It's the very thing!" he shouted. "A back fire! Why didn't I think of it before? We must set a line of it as quick as we can!"

Worth did not understand, and hesitated; but seeing Sumner, with a bunch of lighted leaves in his hand, rush from one clump of palmetto to another, touching his blazing torch to their dry, tinderlike stalks, he realized that his companion knew what he was about, and began to follow his example.

Within five minutes a wall of flame a hundred yards in length was roaring and leaping in front of them, fanned into such fury by the high wind that they were obliged to retreat from its blistering breath. They could not retreat far, however, for during their delay the main fire had gained fearfully upon them, and its awful roar seemed one of rage that they should have attempted to escape from it. Mingled with this was the crash of falling trees and the screams of wild animals that now began to rush frantically past the boys. A herd of flying deer nearly trampled them underfoot; and directly afterwards they were confronted with the gleaming eyes of a panther. With an angry snarl he too dashed forward. Great snakes writhed and hissed along the ground, and Worth clutched Sumner's arm in terror.

Seizing his gun, the latter began shooting at the snakes; nor did he stop until his last cartridge was expended.

It was horrible to stand there helplessly awaiting the result of that life-and-death race between those mighty columns of flame; but they knew not what else to do. Now they could no longer see in which direction to fly. The swirling smoke-clouds were closing in on them from all sides, and only by holding their faces close to the earth could they catch occasional breaths of fresh air.

Sumner's plan was to remain where they were

until the last moment, and then rush out over the smouldering embers of the fire they had set. The main body of this was now rapidly retreating from them. At the same time a fringe of flame from it was working backward towards them. Though they made feeble efforts to beat this out, their strength was too nearly exhausted for them to make much headway against it. The heat was now so intense that their skin was blistering, and their brains seemed almost ready to burst.

Worth had flung away his gun, just after loading it, when he began to set the back fires, and now the sound of a double report from that direction showed that the flames had found it. The noise of these reports was followed by a loud cry, and out of the smoke-clouds a strange, wild figure came leaping. It was a human figure. As the boys recognized it, they echoed its cry. Then by their frantic shouts they guided it to where they were crouching and making ready for their desperate rush into the hot ashes and still blazing remains of the back fire.

The figure that sprang to their side, and, seizing Worth's arm, uttered the single word "Come!" was that of Ul-we, the young Seminole, though the boys, having never seen him, did not, of course, recognize him.

With thankful hearts and implicit faith they followed him as he dashed back into the thickest of the smoke-clouds that still hung low over the newly burnt space before them. They choked and gasped, and their feet became blistered with the heat that penetrated through the soles of their boots. Worth would have fallen but for the strong hand that upheld him, and dragged him resistlessly forward. The ordeal of fire lasted but a minute, when they emerged in a grassy glade at one end of the burnt space, and ran to a clump of water-loving shrubs that marked a slough beyond it.

The vanguard of the main fire raced close after them, flashing through the brittle grass as though it were gunpowder; and as they dashed into the bushes, and their feet sank into the mud and water of the slough, its hot breath was mingled with theirs.

In the very centre of the thicket Ul-we threw himself down in water that just covered his body, and held his head a little above its surface. The boys followed his example, and experienced an instant relief from the cool water. In this position they could breathe easily, for the smoke-clouds seemed unable to touch the surface of the water, but rolled two or three inches above it.

Here they lay for what seemed an eternity while the fire-fiends raged and roared on all sides of them, and in the air above. The heat waves scorched and withered the green thicket, the water of the little slough grew warm and almost hot, the air that they breathed was stifling, and for a time it almost seemed as though they had escaped a roasting only to be boiled alive like lobsters.

After a while, that appeared to the poor boys a long, weary time, the fiercest of the flames swept by, and their roar no longer filled the surrounding space. There were rifts in the smoke-clouds, and perceptible intervals of fresh air between them. Finally the boys could sit up, and at length stand, but not until then were they certain that the danger had passed.

Then Sumner grasped the young Indian's right hand in both of his, and tears stood in the boy's eyes as he said: "I don't know as you can understand me; I don't know who you are, and I don't care. I only know that you have saved us from a horrible death, and that from this moment I am your friend for life."

As for poor Worth, the tears fairly streamed down his smoke-begrimed, blood-stained cheeks, as, in faltering words, he also tried to express his gratitude.

"THE ORDEAL OF FIRE LASTED BUT A MINUTE."

… A Story of the Everglades.

The Indian seemed to understand, for he smiled and said: "Me Ul-we. Quor'm know um. You Summer. You Worf. Me heap glad find um. 'Fraid not. Hunt um; hunt um long time, no find um. Bimeby hear gun, plenty. Hunt um, no find um. Bimeby hear one gun, bang! bang! quick. Then come, find um. *Hindleste*. If me no find um, fire catch um pretty quick, burn up, go big sleep *Holewagus!* Ul-we feel bad, Quor'm feel bad, all body feel bad. Now all body heap hap, dance, sing, eat heap, feel plenty glad."

All of which may be translated thus: "I am very glad to have found you, for I was afraid I shouldn't. I hunted and hunted a long time, but couldn't find you. At last I heard guns fired many times, and hunted in that direction, still without finding you. Finally I heard both barrels of a gun fired at once, not far from where I was, and then I found you. It is good. If I had not found you just when I did, the fire would have caught you and burned you to death, which would have been terrible. I should have felt very badly. So would Quorum and all your friends. Now everybody will rejoice."

Ul-we had been ordered to watch the camp of the white men by the river until they left it, but to remain unseen by them. He had noted the departure of the hunting party, and had also been aware of the approach of the forest fire while it was still at a great distance. When, some hours later, the Lieutenant came back full of anxiety concerning the boys, and immediately started off again to hunt for them, Ul-we also started in another direction, with the happy result already described.

They remained in the slough two hours longer, before the surrounding country was sufficiently cooled off for them to travel over it. Then they set out under Ul-we's guidance, though where he would take them to the boys had not the faintest idea.

Chapter XXXV.

THE BOYS IN A SEMINOLE CAMP.

ALTHOUGH Ul-we started out from the slough that had proved such a haven of safety in one direction, he quickly found cause to change it for another. This cause was the lameness of the boys, for their blistered feet felt as though parboiled, and each step was so painful that it seemed as if they could not take another. They were also faint for want of food, and exhausted by their recent terrible experience. The young Indian was also suffering greatly. The moccasins had been burned from his feet, and the act of walking caused him the keenest pain; but no trace of limp or hesitation betrayed it, nor did he utter a murmur of complaint.

He had intended leading them directly to their own camp; but that was miles away, and seeing that they would be unable to reach it in their present condition, he changed his course towards a much nearer place of refuge. He soon found that to get Worth even that far he must·support and almost carry him. As for Sumner, he clinched his teeth, and mentally vowing that he would hold out as long as the barefooted Indian, he strode manfully along behind the others with his gun, which he had retained through all their struggles, on his shoulder.

In this way, after an hour of weary marching, they entered a live-oak hammock, into which even the fierce forest fire had not been able to penetrate. Here they were soon greeted by a barking of dogs that announced the presence of some sort of a camp. It was that of the Seminole party which had been detailed to conduct our explorers across the Everglades, and act as guards about their halting-places. There were about twenty men in this party, and as they had brought their women and children with them, and had erected at this place a number of palmetto huts, the camp presented the aspect of a regular village. Poor Worth had just strength enough to turn to Sumner, with a feeble smile, and say, "At last we are going to see one," when he sank down, unable to walk another step.

A shout from Ul-we brought the inmates of the camp flocking to the spot. Both the boys were tenderly lifted in strong arms and borne to one of the huts, where they were laid on couches of skins and blankets. They were indeed spectacles calculated to move even an Indian's heart to pity. Their clothing was in rags, while their faces, necks, and hands were torn by the saw-palmettoes through which they had forced their way. Worth was found to have received several cuts from the sharp hoofs of the wounded deer, and he was blood-stained from head to foot. Besides this, they were begrimed with smoke and soot until their original color had entirely disappeared. They were water-soaked and plastered with mud and ashes. Certainly two more forlorn and thoroughly wretched-looking objects had never been seen there, or elsewhere, than were our canoemates at that moment.

But no people know better how to deal with just such cases than the Indians into whose hands the boys had so fortunately fallen, and within an hour their condition was materially changed for the better. Their soaked and ragged clothing had been removed, they had been bathed in hot water and briskly rubbed from head to foot. A salve of bear's grease had been applied to their cuts and to their blistered feet, which latter were also bound with strips of cotton-cloth. Each was clad in a clean calico shirt of gaudy colors and fanciful ornamentation. Each had a gay handkerchief bound about his head, and a pair of loose moccasins drawn over his bandaged feet. Each was also provided with a red blanket which, belted about the waist and hanging to the ground, took the place of trousers.

Thus arrayed, and sitting on bear-skin couches, with a steaming sofkee kettle and its great wooden spoon between them, it is doubtful if their own parents would have recognized them. For all that they were very comfortable, and by the way that sofkee was disappearing, it was evident that their appetites at least had suffered no injury. They at once recognized sofkee from Quorum's description. They also knew the history of the wooden spoon; but just now they were too hungry to remember it, or to care if they did.

At length, when they had almost reached the limit of their capacity in the eating line, and began to find time for conversation, Worth remarked, meditatively:

"I believe, after all, that I like fishing better than hunting. There isn't so much excitement about it, but, on the whole, I think it is more satisfactory."

"Fishing for what?" laughed Sumner. "For bits of meat, with a wooden spoon, in a Seminole sofkee kettle, and looking so much like an Indian that your own father would refuse to recognize you?"

"If I thought I looked as much like an Indian

as you do I would never claim to be a white boy again," retorted Worth.

"I only wish that I could hold a mirror up in front of you," replied Sumner; and then each was so struck by the comical appearance of the other that they laughed until out of breath; while the stolid-faced Seminole boys, stealthily staring at them from outside the hut, exchanged looks of pitying amazement.

After this, Sumner still further excited the wonder of the young Indians by performing several clever sleight-of-hand tricks, while Worth regretted his inability to dance a clog for their benefit. Then calling Ul-we into the hut, Sumner presented him with his shot-gun, greatly to the "Tall One's" satisfaction. Worth was distressed that he had nothing to give the brave young fellow; but brightened at Sumner's suggestion that perhaps Ul-we would go with them to Cape Florida, where Mr. Manton would be certain to present him with some suitable reward for his recent service.

When Ul-we was made to comprehend what was wanted of him, he explained that it would be impossible to go with them then, but that he would meet them at Cape Florida on any date that they might fix. So Sumner fixed the date as the first night of the next new moon, and Worth added a request that he should bring with him all the occupants of the present camp, which he promised to do, if possible.

Although the boys had no idea of where they were, they felt confident that somehow or other they would be able to keep the appointment thus made, and also that the Mantons' yacht would be on hand about the same time. They tried to find out from Ul-we how far they were from Cape Florida at the present moment; but he, having received orders not to afford any member of Lieutenant Carey's party the slightest information regarding the country through which they were passing, pretended not to understand the boys' questions, and only answered, vaguely, "Un-cah" to all of them.

By this time the day was nearly spent, and it was sunset when the boys' own clothes were returned to them, dried, cleaned, and with their rents neatly mended by the skilful needles of the Seminole squaws. Then Ul-we said he was ready to take them to their own camp, and though they would gladly have stayed longer in this interesting village, the boys realized that they ought to relieve Lieutenant Carey's anxiety as soon as possible. So they expressed their willingness to accompany Ul-we, but hoped that the walk would not be a long one.

"No walk," replied Ul-we, smiling. "Go Injun boat. Heap quick."

Accompanied by half the camp, and shouting back, "Heep-a-non-est-cha," which they had learned meant good-bye, to the rest, they followed their guide a short distance to the head of a narrow ditch that had evidently been dug by the Indians. Here they entered Ul-we's canoe, and after a few minutes of poling they realized, in spite of the darkness, that they were once more on the edge of the Everglades.

After skirting the forest line for some time, they turned sharply into a stream that entered it, and again the boys found themselves borne rapidly along on a swift current through a cypress belt. An hour later they saw the glow of a camp-fire through the trees, and their canoe was directed towards it. Stepping out as the canoe slid silently up to the bank, the boys, wishing to surprise their friends, stole softly in the direction of the circle of firelight. On its edge they paused.

At one side of the fire sat Lieutenant Carey, looking worn and haggard; Quorum stood near him, gazing into the flames with an expression of the deepest dejection, while the sailor, looking very solemn, was toasting a bit of fresh meat on the end of a stick.

"No," they heard the Lieutenant say, "I can't conceive any hope that they have escaped, for the only traces that I found of them led directly towards the fire. How I can ever muster up courage to face Mrs. Rankin or meet the Mantons with the news of this tragedy, I don't know."

"Hit's a ter'ble ting, sah. Ole Quor'm know him couldn' do hit."

"Then it's lucky you won't have to try!" exclaimed Sumner, joyously, stepping into sight, closely followed by Worth.

"Oh, you precious young rascals! You villains, you!" cried the Lieutenant, springing to his feet, and seizing the boys by the shoulders, as though about to shake them. "How dared you give us such a fright? Where have you been?"

"Out deer-hunting, sir," answered Sumner, demurely.

Quorum was dancing about them, uttering uncouth and inarticulate expressions of joy; while the sailor, having dropped his meat into the fire, where it burned unheeded, gazed at them in speechless amazement.

They told their story in disjointed sentences, from which their hearers only gathered a vague idea that they had killed a deer in the burning forest, been rescued from the flames by an Indian, and borne in his arms to a Seminole village

in the Everglades, from which, by some unseen means, they had just come.

"I'll bring him up, and he can tell you all about it himself," concluded Sumner, turning towards the landing-place, to which the Lieutenant insisted on accompanying him, apparently not willing to trust him again out of sight.

But neither Ul-we nor his canoe was there. He had taken advantage of the momentary confusion to disappear, and the Lieutenant said he was thankful their canoes had not disappeared at the same time.

When they returned to the fire, they found Quorum hard at work cooking venison steaks.

"Then you did get a deer, sir, after all?" queried Sumner.

"No, I only wounded one, and he escaped. This fellow was one of a herd that, terrified by the fire, came crashing right into camp, and was shot by the sailor."

"That's the way I shall hunt hereafter," exclaimed Worth — "stay quietly and safely in camp, and let the game come to me!"

Chapter XXXVI.

ONE OF THE RAREST ANIMALS IN THE WORLD.

AFTER their day of excitement, terror, and anxiety the explorers passed a happy evening around their camp-fire, and Lieutenant Carey gained a clearer idea of the boys' adventures and escapes. He admitted that the kindness shown them in the Seminole camp gave him a new insight into the Indian character, and wished that he might have had a chance to thank and reward Ul-we for his brave rescue of the young canoemates. He also regretted that he, too, could not have visited that Indian camp, and hoped that the appointment made by the boys with Ul-we might be kept.

In spite of their recent hearty meal of sofkee, a preparation of which they spoke in the highest terms, the boys were able to do ample justice to Quorum's venison steaks, greatly to the satisfaction of the old negro. He would have felt deeply grieved if they had allowed any amount of feasting in an Indian camp to interfere with their enjoyment of a meal that he had cooked,

A Story of the Everglades.

no matter how short an interval might have elapsed between the two.

Although the boys felt rather stiff and lame the next morning, it did not prevent their being ready bright and early to continue their journey. It was a great pleasure to be once more afloat in their own canoes, and this was increased by the fact that they now had a swift current with them. It was a glorious March day, and all nature seemed to share their high spirits as they glided smoothly down the beautiful river. The water swarmed with fish and alligators, and the adjacent forest was alive with birds. Among the innumerable fish that darted beneath them, they soon recognized several salt-water varieties, which assured them that the ocean could not be far off.

As the three canoes were moving quietly along abreast of each other and close together, the *Psyche* suddenly glided over a huge black object that for an instant seemed inclined to rise and lift it bodily into the air. As it was dropped back, there was a tremendous floundering, and all three of the light craft were rocked so violently that only the skill of their navigators saved them from capsizing.

"Was it a waterquake?" inquired Worth, with a very pale face, as soon as his fright would allow him to speak.

"Yes; and there it goes," laughed the Lieutenant, pointing to a great dim form that could just be seen moving swiftly off through the clear water.

"It must have been a whale," said Sumner.

"No," answered Lieutenant Carey; "but it was the next thing to it. It was a manatee or sea-cow. I have seen them in the lower Indian River, but did not know they were found down here. I wish you boys might have a good look at him, though, for the manatee is one of the rarest animals in the world. It is warm-blooded and amphibious, lives on water-grasses and other aquatic plants, grows to be twelve or fifteen feet long, weighs nearly a ton, and is one of the most timid and harmless of creatures. It is the only living representative of its family on this continent, all the other members being extinct. The Indians hunt it for its meat, which is said to be very good eating, and for its bones, which are as fine-grained and as hard as ivory. In general appearance it is not unlike a seal. It can strike a powerful blow with its great flat tail, but is otherwise unarmed and incapable of injuring an enemy. Several have been caught in nets and shipped North for exhibition, but none of them has lived more than a few weeks in captivity."

"What made that fellow go for us if he isn't a fighter?" asked Worth.

"He didn't," laughed the Lieutenant. "He was probably asleep, and is wondering why we went for him. I can assure you that he was vastly more scared than we were."

"He must have been frightened almost to death, then," said Sumner.

Soon after this they saw a landing-place on the left bank. Stopping to examine it, they discovered a trail leading through a fringe of bushes, behind which was an Indian field covering an old shell mound, and in a high state of cultivation. In it were growing sweet-potatoes, melons, squashes, sugar-cane, and beans—a supply of which they would gladly have purchased had the proprietors been present. As they were not, and necessity knows no law, our canoemen helped themselves to what they needed, and when they left, the load of the cruiser was materially increased.

At length they heard the dull boom of surf, and realized that only a narrow strip of land separated them from the ocean. Late in the afternoon they reached the mouth of the river, and the boys uttered joyous shouts as they looked out over its bar and saw a limitless expanse of blue waters, unbroken by islands, glistening in the light of the setting sun.

With light hearts they went into camp on the inner side of the sandy point separating the quiet waters on which they had been floating from the long swells of the open sea. They intended running out of the river and down the coast in the morning, for from their surroundings, as well as from the general course they had taken through the 'Glades, the Lieutenant was satisfied that they must be considerably to the north of Cape Florida.

The boys determined to sleep in their canoes that night, and rigged up the little-used striped canoe tents for that purpose. While they were doing this, and the Lieutenant was pitching his own tent on shore, and the others were collecting drift-wood on the beach, there came a hail from across the river.

"Hello there! Bring a boat over here, can't ye?"

It was the first white man they had seen since leaving the *Transit*, and going over in the cruiser, Sumner brought him back. He proved to be a barefooted boy, a year younger than Worth, and yet he was the mail-carrier over the most southerly land route, and one of the most lonesome, in the United States. It is the seventy-mile stretch between Lake Worth and Biscayne Bay, and every week this boy or his younger brother walked the whole distance and back along the beach, with a mail-sack on his back. He had to cross the mouths of two rivers, for which purpose he kept an old skiff at each one. It sometimes happened, as in the present case, that some other beach traveller would appropriate his boat, and leave it on the wrong side. Then, unless fortunate enough to find some one to set him across, he would be obliged to brave the sharks and other sea-monsters, with which these rivers swarm, and swim over after his own boat. Along his route were three houses of refuge, situated twenty miles apart, and belonging to the Life-saving Service. Each of them contained a single keeper, and these were the only persons seen by the lonely mail-boy while on his toilsome tramps.

The boy was greatly interested in the canoes, which he declared were the neatest little tricks he ever did see, but he scouted the idea of sleeping in them. "Why," said he, "some of them sharks or porpusses what uses round here nights will run inter ye an' upsot ye quicker'n wink."

He was amazed that they should cruise in such tiny craft, and begged them not to think of attempting to run down the coast in them. On the whole he regarded our young canoemates as being particularly daring and reckless fellows, and they regarded him in much the same way, though he made light of his lonely beach tramps, on which he often met bears, panthers, or other wild animals.

He told them that they were about twenty-five miles north of Cape Florida; that there was a "station" on the beach six miles north of them; that turtle were beginning to lay eggs, and bears to frequent the beach in search of them; that sharks grew larger in those very waters than anywhere else on the coast; and that an easterly wind would blow in the morning, which would prevent their crossing the bar. Having delivered himself of this information, and saying that he must make the station that night, the boy slung his mail-sack over his shoulders, and started off at a brisk pace up the soft shelving beach.

After what he had told them about sharks, Sumner and Worth concluded not to sleep in their canoes that night. They might have done so with perfect safety, however, for no shark was ever known to overturn a boat for the sake of getting at a human being inside of it.

The next morning the mail-boy's prediction in regard to the east wind was verified. It was blowing briskly at sunrise, and already a big sea was rolling in, combing and booming on the bar. Their boats would not live in it a moment, and consequently they must stay where they were until the wind changed.

After breakfast the Lieutenant sat in his tent writing, the sailor was repairing a torn sail,

Quorum was taking a nap, and the boys were left to their own devices for amusement. An hour or so later Lieutenant Carey, the sailor, and Quorum were startled by loud calls for help from the beach, and hurried in that direction to see what new scrape the "young rascals," as the Lieutenant called them, had got into now.

Chapter XXXVII.

FISHING FOR SHARKS.

In strolling along the outer beach, picking up curious sponges and bits of coral, the attention of the boys was also attracted to the shadowy forms of great fish that they could distinguish every now and then darting along the green base of the combers just before they broke.

"Do you think they can be sharks?" asked Worth.

"Yes," replied Sumner; "I am almost sure they are."

"My! but I wish we could catch one! I have never seen a shark out of water."

"I shouldn't wonder if we could. I've got a shark-hook in the *Psyche*, and our Manila cables, knotted together, will make just the kind of line we want."

Fifteen minutes later the hook and line had been prepared. For bait, they took one of a number of fish that Quorum had caught that morning.

The shark-hook was a huge affair, over a foot

long and made of steel a quarter of an inch thick. To it was attached by a swivel several feet of chain terminating in a ring to which the line was made fast.

Sumner had caught many sharks off Key West wharves, but they had been comparatively small, and with the monsters of the reef he had hitherto had no dealings. Consequently, he was almost as ignorant of their strength as was Worth. Therefore, without reflecting on the folly of the act, and fearing that the line might be jerked from his hands, he made its inner end fast about his waist.

Then whirling the heavy hook above his head, he cast it far out in the breakers. Within a minute it was tossed back to the beach, and had to be thrown again. This operation was repeated so many times without any result that the boys were beginning to tire of it, when all at once there came a jerk on the line that nearly threw Sumner off his feet.

"Hurrah!" he cried. "We've got him at last! Catch hold, Worth, and help me haul him in."

But it was soon evident that instead of their catching the shark, he had caught them. In spite of all their efforts, and no matter how deeply they dug their feet into the sand, the boys found themselves being dragged slowly but surely towards the water. At first they did not realize their danger; but when they were within a few yards of the creamy froth churned up by the breakers, it flashed over them, and they began to utter those shouts for help that attracted the attention of their companions in the camp.

Although Worth could have let go of the line at any minute, the thought of doing such a thing never entered his head. Even when the water was about his feet and the wet sand was slipping rapidly from beneath them, the plucky little chap held on and struggled with all his might to avert the fate that threatened his friend.

They were nearly hopeless before the three men reached them, and, rushing into the water, seized the line with such a powerful grasp that its seaward motion was instantly arrested. Not only that, but they walked away with it so easily that a minute later the shark was landed high and dry on the beach, where the sailor despatched it with an axe.

It was a white shark of moderate size, being not more than seven or eight feet long. For all that, it was a monster as compared with those Sumner had been in the habit of catching, and he gazed with a curious sensation at its wicked eyes, and the row upon row of curved gleaming teeth with which the gaping mouth was provided.

"It was a close call for you, my boy," said the Lieutenant, gravely, "and has taught you a lesson that I am sure you will never forget. You may thank your lucky stars that the hook was taken by this little fellow instead of by one of his grandfathers or uncles. Now that we have started in this business, I am going to try and show you what might have happened."

Under his direction a hole some five feet deep was dug, a heavy timber, selected from those with which the beach was strewn, was thrust into it, and the sand was repacked solidly about it. To this, instead of to Sumner's body, the end of the line was attached, and the fishing for sharks was resumed. While the post was being set, Lieutenant Carey brought his rifle from the camp. Several sharks, some smaller and some larger than the first, were caught; but not until the hook was seized by one that dragged the entire party clinging to it slowly down the beach did the Lieutenant express himself as satisfied.

"Hold on to it!" he cried. "Brace yourselves! Snub him all you can!"

The strain on the line was tremendous, and it hummed like a harpstring. But for the post to aid them, they must have let go. At length, even the enormous strength at the other end of the line began to be exhausted. Foot by foot the slack was gathered in and held at the post. Then a great ugly-looking head could be seen in the edge of the breakers, and the next minute a rifle-ball crashed into it.

In the flurry that followed the line snapped, and the boys uttered a cry of dismay. But the bullet had done its work, and a few minutes later the huge carcass was rolling like a log in the surf. The sailor managed to get a bight of the line over its tail, and by their united efforts the great fish was drawn partly from the water; but beyond there they could not move it. It was nearly fifteen feet long, and Sumner shuddered as he realized how easily and quickly such a monster as that could have dragged him out to sea.

"It seems to me," said Worth, "that some kinds of fishing are as dangerous as deer-hunting, and just as exciting."

While they were still looking at the big shark their attention was attracted to a loud barking in the beach scrub behind them, and by a man's voice shouting: "Wus-le! Wus-le! You, sir! Come here!" It was evident that Wus-le was a dog, and that he was engaged in some absorbing occupation that forbade him to pay any attention to the calls of his unseen master.

Going to the place from which the barking came, the shark-fishers were in time to witness a

A Story of the Everglades.

most interesting performance. A small brindled bull-terrier was tearing in a circle round and round a coiled rattlesnake. The former was barking furiously, and the sound so enraged the snake that the angry whir-r-r-r of its rattles was almost continuous. At the same time it was dazed by the rapidity of the dog's motions. At length it sprang forward, struck viciously, and missed its mark. At the same moment the dog dashed in, seized the snake by the back, gave one furious shake, and jumped away. The snake was evidently injured, for it re-coiled slowly. Once more, enraged beyond endurance, it struck at its agile adversary, and then the dog had him. In an instant the snake's back was broken, and a minute later it lay motionless and dead.

As soon as he was certain of his victory, the dog paid no more attention to his late enemy, but with panting breath and lolling tongue that betrayed the energy of his recent exertions, he ran to meet his master, who appeared at that moment from the direction of the river.

He was a powerfully built man, dressed partly as a hunter and partly as a sailor. He carried a rifle, and introduced himself as the keeper of the house of refuge a few miles up the coast. He upbraided the dog as though it were a human being for tackling a rattlesnake, and then remarked apologetically to the spectators of the recent fight: "I have to scold him on general principles, but it don't do any good. He is bound to fight and kill snakes till they kill him, which I am always expecting they will. They haven't done it yet, though, and he has killed more than twenty rattlers, besides more of other kinds than I can count. He's a good dog, Wus-le is, and he's a terror to snakes."

The man said he had learned of the Lieutenant and his companions being in the river from the mail-carrier, and, feeling lonely, had come to invite them to go to the station and stay with him until the wind changed. As he assured them that this was not likely to happen for several days, and as they were ahead of the time set for their arrival at Cape Florida, Lieutenant Carey accepted the invitation.

On their way up the river their guide pointed out a grove of cocoanut-palms, marking the site of a fort erected during the Seminole War, the name of which was at one time familiar to all Americans. It was the scene of the treacherous seizure of the famous chief Osceola, who was lured into it under the pretence of considering a treaty. From there he was hurried to Fort Moultrie, in Charleston Harbor, where he soon afterwards died of a broken heart.

They found the station to be a low, roomy structure, surrounded by broad piazzas, built in the most solid manner so as to withstand hurricanes. It stood on top of the beach ridge, and commanded a glorious view of the ocean, as well as of the low-lying back country. At one end was a small separate house containing a great cistern, in which a supply of water was collected during the rainy season of summer, to last through the long winter drought. At the opposite end stood a building in which was kept a metallic life-boat and a quantity of canned provisions for the use of sailors who might be wrecked on that lonely coast.

Here the exploring party remained for nearly a week, while the wind still held steadily to the east, and they all declared it to be the happiest and most interesting week of their cruise.

They hunted, fished, and sailed on the inland waters behind the beach ridge to their hearts' content. Quorum was kept constantly busy cooking on the station kitchen stove the venison, fish, turtle, ducks, quail, 'possum, and other food supplies with which the surrounding country abounded.

Worth felt that his reputation as a hunter was fully restored when he shot a wild-cat that Wus-le had treed, and Sumner was more than proud over the killing of a black bear, which the same enterprising dog discovered one night digging for turtle eggs on the beach but a short distance from the station. The Lieutenant worked at the report of his expedition, while the sailor and the keeper labored at the frame of a light-draught, sea-going boat, which the latter wished to build for his own use, and for which Sumner furnished the plans and model.

At length the wind, which in that country always boxes the compass, worked around to the westward, and as it was the end of March, the canoes were again loaded, and the pleasant life at the station came to an end.

Chapter XXXVIII.

LITTLE KO-WIK-A SAILS OUT TO SEA.

There was a long swell heaving in over the bar at the mouth of the river, but no breakers; and the little fleet, crossing it easily, laid a course down the coast. A stretch of twenty miles lay before them ere they would find another opening into which they could run for shelter, and they were therefore desirous of making the run before night. On most waters this would not have been difficult; but just here was a strong head current, that of the Gulf Stream, running fully three miles an hour, and they knew that to overcome this, and also to make twenty miles during the day, would tax the sailing powers of their small craft to the utmost. Nor could they all sail. The *Hu-la-lah* had no centre-board, and with the wind somewhat forward of abeam, the use of her sail would only have driven her off shore. The Lieutenant was therefore obliged to rely upon his paddle and keep close to the coast. The cruiser, being a slow sailer close-hauled, kept him company, but the *Psyche* and *Cupid* drew gradually ahead, and were soon out of hailing distance.

It was so delightful to find themselves again sailing, and their canoes were doing so splendidly, that the boys hated to stop. And why should they? There was nothing to fear. They knew where they were going, the others were in company, and a halting-place for the night had been agreed upon. They would stop when they reached it, and that would be soon enough.

Until noon the breeze was very light, but after that it freshened and soon came off the land in angry little gusts that suggested the propriety of reefing. With a single reef in each of their sails, they ran until late in the afternoon, when they sighted a cut leading into the great landlocked sheet of Biscayne Bay. They were to enter this bay and cruise down behind its outer keys to Cape Florida, but it had been decided that they should camp on the upper side of the cut for that night.

The wind had increased in strength until now even double-reefed sails could hardly be carried on the canoes. The whole sky was covered with dark clouds, while a bank of inky blackness was rising in the west. It was evident that a windsquall of unusual violence would shortly burst upon them, and almost at the same moment both the canoemates lowered their sails, jointed their paddles, and headed straight in for land. As he lowered his sail and cast a glance astern in search of the other boats, Sumner noticed a large steamer coming down the coast. He wondered if she were not too close in for safety, but the immediate demands of his situation quickly drove all thoughts of her from his mind.

In the teeth of the spiteful gusts, and facing the ominous blackness, they worked their way in until they could see the very place that the station-keeper had described to them as being a suitable camping-ground. Five minutes more would take them to its shelter. Just then Sumner shouted to Worth, and drew his attention to a strange craft that he had been watching for several minutes. It was coming out of the cut, running dead before the wind, but yawing and gybing in a manner that indicated either utter recklessness or absolute ignorance on the part of its crew. The two canoes were so close together that Worth could hear Sumner plainly as he shouted:

"It's an Indian canoe, and apparently unmanageable. I'm going to up sail and run down for a look at it. Do you paddle in to shore, and be out of harm's way before that squall bursts."

"Oh, Sumner, don't run any risks!" shouted Worth.

"All right, I'll be careful. But you'll make things a great deal easier for me if you will start at once for shore. That's a good fellow."

So Worth did as his friend desired, and Sumner, hoisting his double-reefed main-sail, bore down on the strange canoe, which would otherwise have passed him at quite a distance. It was going at a tremendous pace, and as the two craft neared each other, Sumner saw to his consternation that the sole occupant of the dugout was a child who stretched out its little arms imploringly towards him. He saw this as the runaway canoe, under full sail, shot across his bow.

A tumult of thought flashed through the boy's mind like lightning. He was near enough to land to reach it in safety. That child, if left alone, was rushing to certain destruction. He might be able to rescue it, and he might not. The chances were that he would lose his own life in the attempt. Very well; could he lose it in a better cause? What would his father have done under similar circumstances? That last question was sufficient. There was no longer any room for argument.

Even during his moment of hesitation the boy had been loosening the reef-line of his main-sail, and simultaneously with his decision a quick pull at the halyard exposed its full surface to the wind. Over heeled the canoe, with Sumner leaning far out on the weather side. Then her head paid off, and under the influence of the first blast of the squall she sprang away like a frightened animal, in the direction taken by the runaway.

That same afternoon a fleet of Indian canoes, containing Ul-we and his companions, had crossed Biscayne Bay from the main-land. Instead of descending the river on which they had left our explorers, they had skirted the edge of the 'Glades to another that flowed into the bay, the secret of which they did not choose to have Lieutenant Carey learn. Although it still lacked a day of new moon, they decided to take advantage of the fair wind, cross the bay, and spend the intervening time in catching and smoking a supply of fish at a point several miles above Cape Florida.

In the canoe with Ul-we was his six-year-old brother, the little Ko-wik-a, who was sometimes allowed to hold the sheet while they were sailing, and who considered himself fully competent to manage the boat alone. However, being very wise in some things, he did not say this nor express in words his longing for a chance to prove his skill. He simply waited for an opportunity that was not long in coming.

After the Indians had pitched their camp,

Ul-we, taking Ko-wik-a with him, went up to the cut to set a net into which fish would run with the flood-tide. Reaching the place, he went into the mangroves to cut some poles, leaving his little brother in the canoe.

This was Ko-wik-a's chance, and he was quick to seize it. He would now show Ul-we that if he was little, he could sail a boat. The big brother had hardly disappeared when the little one shoved the canoe out from the mangroves and grasped the sheet in his chubby hands. The sail was already hoisted. He did not try to steer, but the wind and swiftly ebbing tide did that for him. A minute later and he was running out of the cut at racing speed, wholly jubilant over the complete success of his experiment. When he got ready to turn round and go back, he became a little frightened to find out that something more than wishing to do so was necessary. When his craft shot out from the cut, and, leaving the land behind, headed out into an infinitely larger body of water than the little fellow had ever before seen, he became thoroughly demoralized, and began to call loudly for Ul-we.

Poor Ul-we had just discovered that both his little brother, whom he loved better than anyone or anything in the world, and his canoe had disappeared, and was rushing frantically towards the outer beach. His instinct told him what had happened, and his one hope was to reach the end of the cut in time to swim off and intercept the runaway.

When he did get there it was only in time to catch a fleeting glimpse of his own well-known sail far out at sea, with another much whiter and smaller one behind it. Then a cruel squall burst over the ocean. In a cloud of rain and mist, borne forward by the fierce wind, the two sails disappeared and the whole landscape was blotted from view.

From a place of safety on the opposite side of the cut, though unseen by Ul-we, Worth Manton strained his eyes for a last glimpse of the *Psyche's* fluttering signal flag, and the others, rapidly nearing him, wondered at his gesture of despair as it was blotted out.

The squall was long and fierce, and by the time it had passed, the darkness of night had shut in and the stars were shining.

Chapter XXXIX.

A BLACK SQUALL AND THE STRANDED STEAMER.

Although the *Psyche* was flying at racing speed dead before the wind, which freshened with each moment, and was rolling frightfully under her press of canvas, she was no match in running for the long dugout of which she was in pursuit. Had the latter been properly trimmed and steered, the light cedar canoe could never have caught it. As it was, Sumner saw that he was gaining, but so slowly that he could not hope to overtake it before being carried miles out to sea. In that weather and with night coming on, this was by no means a cheerful prospect. Still he had no thought of turning back. He had entered upon this race with a full knowledge of its possible consequences, and he would either save the helpless little figure that had appealed to him so imploringly, or perish with it.

So the clutch on his deck tiller tightened, and the taut main-sheet held in the other hand was not slackened a single inch, until the hissing

A Story of the Everglades.

rush of the black squall was in his ears. Then the canoe was sharply luffed, the sheet was dropped, the halyard cast off, and the white sail fell to the deck like a broken wing. As it was gathered in and made fast with a turn of the sheet, the squall burst on the stanch little craft and heeled it far over. It offered too little resistance to be capsized, and a minute later, steadied by the double-bladed paddle, it was once more got before the wind and was scudding under bare poles.

While doing all this, Sumner had been too busy to look after the object of his pursuit. Now he could not see it, and he almost choked with the thought that his brave effort had been made in vain, after all. No, there it was, close at hand, but no longer showing a sail or flying from him. Heeling over before the blast, its long boom had been thrust into the water, and in an instant the slender craft had been upset. Now, full of water, it floated on one side like a log. At first, Sumner failed to see its tiny occupant, and the thought that he had been drowned almost within reach was a bitter one. But no. Hurrah! There he is! With head just above the water, and chubby hands clutching at the slippery sides of his craft, the plucky little chap was still fighting for life.

As the *Psyche* swept alongside, steered to a nicety, Sumner reached out, and, nearly overturning his canoe by the effort, caught the little fellow by an arm. The water was pouring in over the cockpit coaming, and had the child been a pound heavier, the next instant would have seen two helplessly drifting canoes instead of one. As it was, he was hauled in and safely deposited in the inch or more of water that swashed above the cockpit floor.

With infinite self-possession the child smiled up into the face of his rescuer and lisped: "How, Sumner!"

Then the boy recognized the little Ko-wik-a, whose acquaintance he had made in Ul-we's camp, and as a relief to his own overstrained nerves, called him a little imp, and abused him roundly for getting them into such a scrape. At the same time tears stood in his eyes, and he could have hugged the child cuddling between his knees and smiling so confidingly in his face.

Though the rescue of Ko-wik-a had been so happily accomplished, they were still in a sad plight—driving out to sea in an egg-shell, with no chance of battling back against the tempest, and the darkness of night enshrouding them. With each moment the storm-lashed waves were mounting higher. All Sumner's skill was re-

quired to prevent the canoe from broaching to and turning over. How much longer would his strength hold out? Already he felt it failing. He would soon become exhausted, and then—

Hark! What was that? The note of a steam-whistle? Yes, and another, and still others, struggling back hoarsely against the wind. Then a light twinkled through the darkness, and directly other lights were outlining a huge black shape right in their track.

Sumner remembered the steamer he had seen just before parting from Worth. Could this be she? What was she doing there, apparently at anchor?

Driving under her stern, a few minutes' hard paddling brought the canoe into the quiet calm of the towering lee. Then Sumner shouted again and again, but the voice of the ship calling for aid in her own distress drowned his cries. After a while the whistle notes ceased, and he shouted again. This time he was heard, and an answering hail came from the deck high above him, "Who is it, and where are you?"

Sumner answered, and in a few minutes a port low down in the ship's side was flung open, and a flood of light poured from it. Two ropes were lowered, and Sumner getting the bights under the bow and stern of his canoe, it, with its occupants, was lifted to the level of the open port. Strong arms first received the little Ko-wik-a, and then helped the young canoeman aboard the steamer.

"Where is your vessel?" demanded the captain, who was among those assembled to witness this unexpected arrival.

"There," answered Sumner, pointing to the *Psyche.*

"You don't mean to say that you are navigating the ocean in that cockle-shell?"

"Yes, I do; though I don't expect I should have navigated it much longer if I hadn't fallen in with you just as I did. How do you happen to be at anchor here, and what were you whistling for?"

"We are not at anchor. We are aground, and I was blowing the whistle in the hope of attracting some vessel or vessels, into which we could lighter our cargo. Now I suppose I shall have to throw it overboard."

"What for?" asked Sumner. "With this offshore wind there won't be any heavy sea, and unless you have stove a hole in her bottom she ought to float with the flood-tide."

"Flood-tide! Isn't it the top of the flood now?" exclaimed the captain.

"No; it's the very last of the ebb, and the flood will give you a couple of feet more water."

"Are you certain of that?"

"Certain."

"Then you are a trump!" cried the captain. "And I'm away out of my reckoning, somehow. Your coming just as you have has undoubtedly saved my cargo, for I should have begun heaving it overboard by this time. You see, I was hugging the coast to escape the force of the Gulf as much as possible, but was keeping a sharp lookout for the red buoy that marks the end of the reef. I can't imagine how we missed it, unless it has gone; but we did, and when Fowey was lighted, I saw that we were too close in shore. I didn't know that we were inside of the reef; but we struck within five minutes after I altered her course, and that was nearly half an hour ago. We don't seem to have hit very hard, and she lies easy without making any water; but she's here to stay, unless, as you say, the floodtide will lift her off. You are certain that this is the last of the ebb?"

"As certain as that I am standing here," answered Sumner, who had a very distinct recollection of how the current had rushed out through the cut.

"Then let us go up into my room and have some supper. There you can tell me how you happened to be out here in such weather with a pickaninny aboard while we wait for the tide."

How safe and comfortable the great ship seemed, after that wild race to sea in a canoe! How the captain and mates and passengers marvelled at Sumner's adventures, and what a pet they all made of little Ko-wik-a. As for that self-possessed young Indian, he accepted all the attentions lavished upon him in the most matter-of-fact manner, and with the utmost composure. He expressed no surprise at anything he saw; but his keen little eyes studied all the details of his novel surroundings, and he stored away scraps of startling information with which to astonish his young Everglade comrades for many a day.

The squall passed and the sea smoothed out its wrinkles soon after the crew of the *Psyche* came aboard, and shortly before midnight the rising tide lifted the great ship gently off the reef. She was backed to a safe distance from it, and there anchored to await the coming of daylight.

Knowing what anxiety his friends and Ko-wik-a's friends must be suffering on their account, Sumner determined to return to them at the earliest possible moment. The first signs of dawn, therefore, found the *Psyche*, with her crew and passenger, once more afloat. A hearty cheer followed the brave little craft as she glided away

A Story of the Everglades. 315

from the great ship, and in less than an hour she was paddled gently up to where the other canoes and the cruiser lay on the beach.

It had been a sad night to the inmates of that lonely camp, and most of its long hours had been spent in a fruitless watching for the return of the well-loved lad, whom most of them had such slight hopes of ever again seeing. Only Worth had faith, and declared that while he did not know how Sumner would manage it, he was confident that he would turn up again all right somehow. Towards morning their anxiety found relief in a troubled sleep, and as Sumner walked into the camp there was none to greet him or note his coming.

"Hello, in the camp!" he shouted. "Here it is almost sunrise and no breakfast ready yet!"

No surprise could be more complete or more joyful than that. Worth was the first to spring to his feet.

"He's come back safe and sound!" he shouted. "Oh, Sumner, I knew you would! I was sure of it, and told them so!"

"The next time I let you away from my side it will only be at the end of a long rope, you young rascal, you!" said the Lieutenant, after the extravagant joy of the first greeting had somewhat subsided.

After an unusually late and happy breakfast, they sailed through the cut and into the beautiful bay to which it led. They soon discovered the camp to which Ko-wik-a belonged, and the canoe that had rescued him had the honor of bearing him to it. He was received with a wondering joy that was none the less real for its lack of extravagant manifestation. As Ul-we took the child from Sumner's arms, he turned his face away to hide the emotion that would be unbecoming in an Indian and a warrior. It was there, however, and the look of intense gratitude that he gave the boy was more expressive than any words that he could have uttered.

Then the Indians broke their camp, and they and the whites sailed away together to the appointed rendezvous on Cape Florida.

Chapter XL.

THE HAPPY ENDING OF THE CRUISE.

ON their entire cruise our young canoemates had not enjoyed a day's run so much as they did this one in company with the Indians who had crossed the Everglades with them, but of whom they had seen so little. The wind was so fair that the boats without centre-boards could sail as well as those with, and the run was a series of match races, of which the *Psyche* and *Cupid* were winners in nearly every case.

As Ul-we's canoe had been lost the night before, the Lieutenant invited both him and the little Ko-wik-a to a sail in the *Hu-la-lah*, and even the self-contained young Indian was compelled to express his admiration of the graceful craft. When he ventured to ask what such a canoe would cost, and the price was named, his face indicated his despair at ever being able to accumulate such a sum, and he murmured:

. "Heap money! Injun no get um."

At Cape Florida, while the camps were being pitched but a short distance from each other, the boys went with Ul-we to set another fish-trap, such as he had been about to prepare when Ko-wik-a ran away with his canoe the day before. The little fellow went with them, but he no longer showed any inclination to go sailing on his own hook. After Ul-we had fixed his trap they went over to a submerged bank that extends southward several miles from the cape. Here, while the boys waded in the shoal water collecting sea porcupines, urchins, tiny squids, bits of live coral, and numberless other marine curiosities, Ul-we was busy gathering and throwing into his canoe a quantity of big greenish shells that looked like so many rocks. When they were ready to go back, and Sumner saw this novel cargo, he exclaimed:

"Good! Now we will have some conch soup for dinner!"

"How do you know?" asked Worth.

"Because here are the conchs, and Ul-we has enough for all of us."

"Those things!" cried Worth, in a tone of disgust. "You surely don't mean that they are good to eat?"

"Yes, I do," laughed Sumner, picking up one of the shells and showing Worth the white meat with which its exquisitely pink interior was filled. "I mean that these fellows can be made into the very best soup I know of."

"Seems to me I have seen that kind of a shell before," said Worth, "but I never knew that any one ever ate their contents."

"Of course you have seen the shells. You will find them in half the farm-houses of the country, where, with the point of the small end cut off, they are used as dinner horns. As for the eating part, you wait till Quorum gives you a chance to test it this evening. If you don't find it fully as good as sofkee, then I shall be mistaken."

The boys had been greatly disappointed at not finding either the Mantons' yacht nor the *Transit* awaiting them at the cape. Several times in the course of the afternoon they climbed to the top of an abandoned light-house tower near their camp, in the hope of sighting a sail bound in that direction. As they did so just before sunset, they saw several far over towards the main-land, but they were too distant for their character to be distinguished.

Never had they seen anything so exquisitely beautiful or so royally gorgeous as that Southern sunset, and they lingered at the top of the tower until the last of its marvellous flame tints had burned out, and the delicate crescent of the new moon was sinking into the 'Glades behind the distant pine-trees of the main-land.

At supper time Worth was introduced to conch

soup, and he agreed with Sumner that it was fully equal to sofkee.

After supper the boys strolled over to the Indian camp, to which Lieutenant Carey was attracted soon afterwards by their shouts of laughter. He did not recognize the boys until they spoke to him, for they had persuaded Ul-we to array them as he had after the forest fire, and they were now in full Indian costume.

In the mean time the distant sails that they had sighted from the top of the old tower had been running across the bay before a brisk breeze, and two vessels had quietly come to anchor just inside the cape. The glow of the camp-fires could be seen from these, and from one of them a boat containing several persons pulled in to the beach. A minute later two gentlemen, whose footsteps were unheard in the sand, stood on the edge of the circle of firelight, and one of them said to the other, in a low and disappointed tone:

"It's only an Indian camp after all, Tracy."

"So it is," replied the other, regretfully. "Still, they may be able to give us some news. Let's go in and inquire."

At that moment the attention of the Indians was equally divided between Sumner, who was apparently accumulating a fortune by taking half-dollars from little Ko-wik-a's mouth and ears, and

Worth, who was attempting to dance what he called a clog with Indian variations, to the music of Lieutenant Carey's whistle. Suddenly little Ko-wik-a, who was nervously excited over Sumner's wonderful performance, uttered a startled cry and sprang to one side, staring into the darkness.

All the others looked in the same direction, and probably the dignified Mr. Manton was never more surprised in his life than when a young Indian bounded to his side, flung his arms about his neck, and called him "Dear father!" His brother was equally amazed when another young Indian sprang to where he was standing, seized his hand, and called him "Mr. Tracy!"

When they discovered, by their voices and by what they were incoherently saying, that these young Indians were not Indians at all, but the very boys of whom they were in search, tanned to the color of mahogany, and dressed in borrowed finery, the surprise and delight of the two gentlemen can better be imagined than described.

"Is it possible," cried Mr. Manton, holding Worth off at arm's-length so that the firelight shone full upon him, "that this can be the pale-faced chap with a cough who left me in St. Augustine a couple of months ago? Why, son, you've grown an inch taller and, I should say, six in breadth!" Then, turning to the other boy, and scanning his features closely, he added: "And is this Sumner Rankin, the son of my old schoolmate Rankin, whom I lost sight of after he went into the navy? My boy, for your father's sake, and for the sake of what you have done for Worth this winter, I want you hereafter to regard me as a father, and continue to act as this boy's elder brother. Ever since Tracy told me of you I have been almost as impatient to meet you as to rejoin Worth, for as schoolmates your father and I were as dear to each other as own brothers."

While this joyful meeting was taking place, a boat from the *Transit* had come ashore, and Ensign Sloe was reporting to Lieutenant Carey. Then the whole party had to sit down where they were, and, surrounded by the grave-faced Indians, tell and listen to as much of the past two months' experience as could be crowded into as many hours.

The Mantons were charmed with Lieutenant Carey, and he with them, while towards Ul-we their gratitude was unbounded. Old Quorum, too, was introduced, and warmly thanked for his fidelity to the young canoemates.

Before the schooners sailed for Key West, which they did the next day, Lieutenant Carey presented Ul-we with the *Hu-la-lah*, and Worth gave him the handsomest rifle in his father's col-

lection, besides promising to send little Ko-wik-a a light canoe for his very own. Mr. Manton and Uncle Tracy between them not only purchased from the Indians, at fabulous prices, the costumes in which they found the boys, but everything else they could think of that would aid in reproducing their present appearance and surroundings for the benefit of their Northern friends. The properties they thus acquired included bear, wolf, panther, and deer skins, and even a sofkee kettle with its great wooden spoon. Besides this, they and the Lieutenant so loaded the Indian canoes with provisions, tobacco, cartridges for their rifles and shot-guns, and other useful things, that this occasion formed a theme for conversation about every camp-fire throughout the length and breadth of the Everglades for many a long day. Should Lieutenant Carey and his party ever care to penetrate those wilds again, they will be certain of a hearty welcome, and of being allowed to go where they please.

Then the two yachts set sail for their run down the reef to Key West, where another joyful greeting awaited the young canoemates.

Before the Mantons left there, it was arranged that Mrs. Rankin should dispose of her Key West home as soon as possible, and sail for New York, where Mr. Manton said he had a cosey little house waiting for just such tenants as herself and Sumner.

"Be sure and come as quickly as you can," he said, "for I want my new boy to design and build me a yacht this summer for next winter's cruising."

"I shall need one too," added Uncle Tracy, "and I think I know of several more that will be wanted."

"Don't forget to bring the *Psyche* with you, Sumner!" shouted Worth, the last thing.

"As if I would!" answered Sumner. "Whatever boats I may own, I will never part with that dear canoe so long as I live."

That evening, as the boy and his mother sat discussing their pleasant prospects for the future, Sumner said:

"Well, mother, I have learned one thing from the past two months' experience, and that is that wealthy people can be just as kind and considerate, and may be as dearly loved, as poor ones. I didn't believe it at one time, but now I know it."

THE END.

www.ingramcontent.com/pod-product-compliance
Lightning Source LLC
Chambersburg PA
CBHW030404230426
43664CB00007BB/739